ommer's™

Buenos Aires
day BY day™

1st Edition

by Neil E. Schlecht

WILEY

John Wiley & Sons Canada, Ltd.

Contents

Published by:

John Wiley & Sons Canada, Ltd.

6045 Freemont Blvd.
Mississauga, ON L5R 4J3

ISBN 978-0-470-16011-4

Editor: Gene Shannon
Production Editor: Pauline Ricablanca
Project Coordinator: Lynsey Stanford
Editorial Assistant: Katie Wolsley
Photo Editor: Photo Affairs, Inc.
Cartographer: Lohnes+Wright
Vice President, Publishing Services: Karen Bryan
Production by Wiley Indianapolis Composition Services

For information on our other products and services or to obtain technical support, please contact our Customer Care Department within the U.S. at 877/762-2974, outside the U.S. at 317/572-3993 or fax 317/572-4002.

Wiley also publishes its books in a variety of electronic formats. Some content that appears in print may not be available in electronic formats.

Manufactured in China

1   2   3   4   5   RRD   13   12   11   10   09

A Note from the Editorial Director

Organizing your time. That's what this guide is all about.

Other guides give you long lists of things to see and do and then expect you to fit the pieces together. The Day by Day guides are different. These guides tell you the best of everything, and then they show you how to see it *in the smartest, most time-efficient way*. Our authors have designed detailed itineraries organized by time, neighborhood, or special interest. And each tour comes with a bulleted map that takes you from stop to stop.

Hoping to learn tango at one of Buenos Aires' famous *milongas* or dine on its world-renowned beef? Planning to visit the final resting place of Evita Perón, take in a *fútbol* match, or sip coffee at one of the city's historic cafés? Whatever your interest or schedule, the Day by Days give you the smartest routes to follow. Not only do we take you to the top attractions, hotels, and restaurants, but we also help you access those special moments that locals get to experience—those "finds" that turn tourists into travelers.

The Day by Days are also your top choice if you're looking for one complete guide for all your travel needs. The best hotels and restaurants for every budget, the greatest shopping values, the wildest nightlife—it's all here.

Why should you trust our judgment? Because our authors personally visit each place they write about. They're an independent lot who say what they think and would never include places they wouldn't recommend to their best friends. They're also open to suggestions from readers. If you'd like to contact them, please send your comments our way at feedback@frommers.com, and we'll pass them on.

Enjoy your Day by Day guide—the most helpful travel companion you can buy. And have the trip of a lifetime.

Warm regards,

Kelly Regan

Kelly Regan, Editorial Director
Frommer's Travel Guides

About the Author

Neil Edward Schlecht has seen Buenos Aires through its ups and downs in the last three decades. He first traveled there in the late 1980s, while living in neighboring Brazil; as Argentina spiraled into hyperinflation, he found himself in a public hospital strapped for supplies, needing local friends to secure x-ray film on the black market. He's happy to report that since then he's witnessed the city come back from the dead a couple of times and transform itself into one of the hottest places on the planet.

A freelance writer and photographer, and the author of *Frommer's Peru, Barcelona Day by Day, Mallorca & Menorca Day by Day,* and many other travel titles, Schlecht resides in rural Litchfield County, Connecticut (USA). He is a huge fan of Argentine wines, but can't dance tango to save his life.

Acknowledgments

To Uisce, who was always waiting for me on my return home. *Y para mis amigos Lau y Sebi. Sin vuestra amistad y ayuda—además de la gentileza de prestarme vuestro hermoso apartamento—hubiera sido mucho menos divertido este proyecto. Gracias y un abrazo muy fuerte.*

An Additional Note

Please be advised that travel information is subject to change at any time—and this is especially true of prices. We therefore suggest that you write or call ahead for confirmation when making your travel plans. The authors, editors, and publisher cannot be held responsible for the experiences of readers while traveling. Your safety is important to us, however, so we encourage you to stay alert and be aware of your surroundings.

Star Ratings, Icons & Abbreviations

Every hotel, restaurant, and attraction listing in this guide has been ranked for quality, value, service, ámenities, and special features using a **star-rating system.** Hotels, restaurants, attractions, shopping, and nightlife are rated on a scale of zero stars (recommended) to three stars (exceptional). In addition to the star-rating system, we also use a **kids icon** to point out the best bets for families. Within each tour, we recommend cafes, bars, or restaurants where you can take a break. Each of these stops appears in a shaded box marked with a coffee-cup-shaped bullet ☕.

The following **abbreviations** are used for credit cards:

AE	American Express	**DISC**	Discover	**V**	Visa
DC	Diners Club	**MC**	MasterCard		

Frommers.com

Now that you have this guidebook to help you plan a great trip, visit our website at **www.frommers.com** for additional travel information on more than 4,000 destinations. We update features regularly to give you instant access to the most current trip-planning information available. At Frommers. com, you'll find scoops on the best airfares, lodging rates, and car rental bargains. You can even book your travel online through our reliable travel booking partners. Other popular features include:

- Online updates of our most popular guidebooks
- Vacation sweepstakes and contest giveaways
- Newsletters highlighting the hottest travel trends
- Podcasts, interactive maps, and up-to-the-minute events listings
- Opinionated blog entries by Arthur Frommer himself
- Online travel message boards with featured travel discussions

A Note on Prices

In the "Take a Break" and "Best Bets" sections of this book, we have used a system of dollar signs to show a range of costs for 1 night in a hotel (the price of a double-occupancy room) or the cost of an entree at a restaurant. Use the following table to decipher the dollar signs:

Cost	Hotels	Restaurants
$	under $100	under $10
$$	$100–$200	$10–$20
$$$	$200–$300	$20–$30
$$$$	$300–$400	$30–$40
$$$$$	over $400	over $40

An Invitation to the Reader

In researching this book, we discovered many wonderful places—hotels, restaurants, shops, and more. We're sure you'll find others. Please tell us about them, so we can share the information with your fellow travelers in upcoming editions. If you were disappointed with a recommendation, we'd love to know that, too. Please write to:

Frommer's Buenos Aires Day by Day, 1st Edition
John Wiley & Sons Canada, Ltd.
6045 Freemont Blvd. • Mississauga, ON L5R 4J3

15 Favorite
Moments

15 Favorite **Moments**

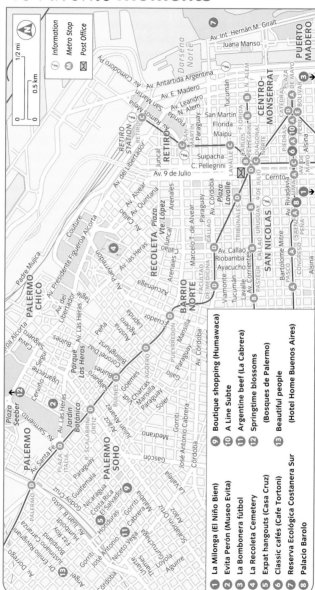

Map Legend
- *i* Information
- Ⓜ Metro Stop
- ☒ Post Office

Previous page: Couple practices tango in an outdoor milonga.

Buenos Aires has become one of the hottest destinations in the world. After yet another economic crisis and currency devaluation made it almost absurdly cheap for non-Argentines, visitors rushed in to discover the most European-looking of South American capitals. And with it, Porteños' (as the locals are called) penchant for massive steaks, fine malbec wines, old cafes, and chic boutiques — and a resurgent national dance, the tango. The following are some of my favorite experiences in the Argentine capital.

1 Reveling in la milonga. Only recently out of fashion, tango is once again the soundtrack to life in Buenos Aires. Chic youngsters and wizened veterans gather at late-night *milongas* in time-worn ballrooms, and whether in jeans or stylish skirts and pumps, they embrace and move to a passionate rhythm unique to Argentina. It's intoxicating to watch, but tango's precise, stylized moves are likely to make novices feel ridiculously clumsy. There are a half-dozen great milongas, but one of the best is El Niño Bien. *See bullet* **9**, *p 118.*

Young Argentines have embraced the tango.

2 Reliving Evita's cult of personality. Evita Perón's (1919–1952) fame hasn't dimmed nearly 60 years after her death. She rose to unexpected power alongside her husband, trade unions, and the

Peronista party, and became a towering national figure, inspiring a Broadway play, a Hollywood movie,

La Recoleta is the resting place of Evita Perón

Café La Perla is one of the city's classic bar notables.

and legions of fans. The city is home to her discrete tomb in Recoleta Cemetery, the Casa Rosada — scene of her famous speeches to Argentine workers — and now the wonderfully personal Evita Museum. *See bullet* ⑩, *p 38.*

③ **Joining the masses — or the elites.** If you're a *fútbol* (soccer) fan, or just a student of group behavior,

The top of Palacio Barolo has stunning panoramic views of the city.

you can't miss an opportunity to attend a match featuring one of Buenos Aires's two top teams. Don war paint in blue and yellow, and root for Boca Juniors at La Bombonera stadium; or wear red and black, and scream for River Plate. Of course, if *fútbol* seems too low-brow, you could always join the jet-set at their favorite springtime diversion, a polo match. *See bullet* ①, *p 24.*

④ **Tiptoeing through a city of the dead.** Stunning La Recoleta Cemetery is the final resting place of Buenos Aires's most elite citizenry, from Presidents and Generals to one Evita Perón. The elaborate tombs are monuments to their achievements and immense family wealth, mausoleums dripping with neo-Classical, Art Nouveau, and Baroque art, topped by somber marble angels and cherubs gazing skyward. *See bullet* ⑫, *p 28.*

⑤ **Getting your expat on.** Buenos Aires suddenly became the new Prague after the peso devaluation in 2002, and though the city is no longer as dirt-cheap as it once was, it's still a value destination full of foreigners living beyond their normal means. Hang out at the most exclusive restaurants and clubs, such as Casa Cruz — where it's fashionable to speak English, Italian, or French — and live it up for a fraction of the cost of New York, Rome, or Paris. *See bullet* ⑮, *p 102.*

⑥ **Drinking in history at a bar notable.** Buenos Aires is renowned for its cafe culture, and many of the city's classic bars and cafes — resonant with a patina of age and events both momentous and small — date from the late 19th and early 20th centuries. The government has protected 53 of them — including the legendary Tortoni — from development's onward march. They're places to sip a *cortado* and take in life at an institution held dear by locals, young and old. *See bullet* ⑦, *p 105.*

⑦ **Leaving the city behind.** Besides its wide avenues and Belle Epoque architecture, Buenos Aires overflows with green spaces. Just behind the towering skyscrapers still going up in Puerto Madero is the Reserva Ecológica Costanera Sur, a reserve of marshland leading down to the muddy Rio de la Plata. The residential neighborhood of Palermo is distinguished by extensive parks and gardens, where Porteños go to show off their toned bodies on a track around a pair of lakes. *See bullet* ①, *p 95.*

⑧ **Zooming to the top of Palacio Barolo.** Mario Palanti's spectacular 1923 neo-Gothic skyscraper is impressive and unique from the street, but if you pop inside, you'll get a treat few Porteños have even experienced. Beyond the sumptuous lobby and gorgeous old-fashioned elevators are upper-floor terraces with stunning panoramic views of all of Buenos Aires. *See bullet* ⑨, *p 48.*

⑨ **Loading up on boutique shopping.** Leather is king in Buenos Aires, of course, so luxurious, handmade bags and shoes are the hot items to score. But you might also come back with a sheepskin rug or gaucho-cool cowhide, bought for a fraction of what they might cost at home. Trendy boutiques in Palermo Viejo, such as Humawaca, are some of the chicest and most visually creative you'll see, meriting a stroll even if you're not buying. *See bullet* ⑮, *p 84.*

⑩ **Riding the A train.** Buenos Aires's subway line is the oldest in South America. The A line, which retains the original 1913 cars that rumble beneath Avenida de Mayo, from the Plaza in front of the Casa Rosada to the House of Congress, is a charming relic, a wood-paneled ride back in time. *See bullet* ②, *p 52.*

⑪ **Attacking Argentine grass-fed beef.** In this land of cattle and wide-open spaces, Argentines live for red meat, which many wolf down at every meal. And that's something in a place where steaks tend to be the

The A line still has original subway cars from 1913.

Jacaranda trees line the city's streets in springtime.

size of the family pet. *Parrilladas* — grilled-meat feasts encompassing virtually every cut of meat you've ever heard of and some you'd never consider eating — are the backbone of the Argentine diet and something carnivores have to experience at a *parrilla* restaurant like La Cabrera. *See bullet* ⑩, *p 105.*

⑫ **Taking in springtime down south.** Hit Buenos Aires in spring, the onset of the dead of winter in the northern hemisphere and one of the best times to visit the city. It turns redolent with the fragrance of jacaranda, jasmine, and magnolia. Wherever you look, trees blossom with the brilliant lavender color of jacarandas and deep-red *ceibo*, the national flower of Argentina. The scene's the best in the wide-open green spaces of the Parque Tres de Febrero. *See bullet* ⑤, *p 90.*

⑬ **Hob-knobbing with la gente bella.** Buenos Aires teems with beautiful people, and restaurants, bars, and shops in the most fashionable districts are the runways where they strut their stuff. Stay in their midst at an uber-cool boutique hotel like Hotel Home Buenos Aires in Palermo Viejo. *See bullet* ①, *p 141.*

⑭ **Playing gaucho at an estancia.** Argentina's famed gaucho culture reigns not more than an hour outside Buenos Aires, in the unendingly flat pampas. Visit a country estate *(estancia)* for the day or spend the night; chow down at a big-time *parrilla;* and visit the tranquil town of San Antonio de Areco, a charming throwback full of exquisite silver craftsmen, colonial buildings, and antique country grocers built around a stately plaza and cobble-stoned streets lined with orange trees. *See p 154.*

⑮ **Going under the knife.** Buenos Aires is full of ridiculously beautiful people, many of whom have been given an assist by plastic surgeons. The city's become a world capital for aesthetic enhancement, so why not get a nose job or breast enhancement while you're down here — or perhaps a tummy tuck after all that beef? (I'm mostly kidding, though you wouldn't be the first to build a vacation to Argentina around, er, a theme of self-improvement.) ●

An antique grocer in San Antonio de Areco.

The Best in **One Day**

i	Information
Ⓜ	Metro Stop
▪	Point of Interest
✉	Post Office

1 Casa Rosada
2 Plaza de Mayo
3 Catedral Metropolitana
4 Cabildo
5 Avenida de Mayo
6 Café Tortoni
7 Av. 9 de Julio/Obelisco
8 Palacio Barolo
9 Palacio del Congreso
10 A Line Subte
11 Plaza San Martin
12 Calle Florida
13 Florida Garden

Previous page: The neighborhood of La Boca is one of the most colorful spots in the city.

This very full one-day tour takes in the best of historic Buenos Aires, and its neighborhoods Monserrat and Retiro, giving you a taste of its beginnings and recent past as one of the wealthiest places on Earth: its famous European-influenced architecture, old-world cafes, and wide avenues, squares, and parks. You'll need walking shoes. START: **Subte to Plaza de Mayo (A) or Catedral (D).**

1 ★★ **Casa Rosada.** Americans have their White House, Argentines their Pink House. At the east end of the Plaza de Mayo, the Argentine presidential palace, where the president works but does not live, is known for its distinctive color (the reason for that hue is a matter of debate and speculation, with some asserting that it was originally painted with cow blood). The asymmetrical building, erected in 1885, is where Evita Perón (1919–1952) addressed her adoring masses (though not from the front balcony, as is usually assumed, but from one on the south side, at Balcarce). In the basement is a presidential museum containing official artifacts once belonging to Argentine presidents over the decades. ⏱ *30 min. Plaza de Mayo (museum entrance at Yrigoyen 219), Monserrat.* ☎ *11/ 4344-3802. www.museo.gov.ar. Free* admission. Mon–Fri 10am–6pm (free guided visits 11am & 3pm); Sun 2–6pm (free guided visits 4pm). Palace tours suspended until completion of renovations. Subte: Plaza de Mayo (A), Bolívar (E), or Catedral (D).

2 ★★ **Plaza de Mayo.** The heart of the historic Monserrat district—and indeed, the entire city—this is the spot where Buenos Aires had its second founding in 1580. The square has been ground zero for virtually every momentous political event in Argentina's modern history, from presidential proclamations to mass protests by Perón's blue-collar workers (the *descamisados,* or shirtless ones) to mournful demonstrations by the "Mothers of the Disappeared," whose children were kidnapped and murdered by the military governments of the 1970s and early 1980s.

The Argentine presidential palace has a distinctive pink hue.

Catedral Metropolitano was completed in 1836 after more than 90 years.

Today, there are still sometimes frequent protests and occasional appearances by the aging *Madres* (mothers)—whose "ownership" of the plaza is marked by the headscarves, their symbol, painted on the tiles around the 1811 obelisk in the center. ⏱ *15 min. Av. de Mayo, Monserrat. Madres de la Plaza de Mayo: every Thurs 3:30pm. Subte: Plaza de Mayo (A), Bolívar (E), or Catedral (D).*

❸ ★ **Catedral Metropolitana.** Over the centuries, beginning in 1622, a half-dozen churches have occupied this spot. The present cathedral's long construction period, from 1745 to 1836, is reflected in its inconsistent appearance, with an austere neo-Classical exterior fronting a gilded, baroque interior. A mausoleum inside contains the remains of General José de San Martín (1778–1850), the national hero and "Father of the Nation" known as *El Libertador* for his campaigns to free the southern nations of South America from Spanish rule. ⏱ *30 min. San Martín (at Rivadavia), Monserrat.* ☎ *11/ 4331-2845. Subte: Plaza de Mayo (A), Bolívar (E), or Catedral (D).*

❹ ★ **Cabildo.** The blindingly white old town hall rests on the spot where the town council first met at the end of the 16th century, and where Argentine independence took root during the May Revolution of 1810. It is the only public building on the Plaza de Mayo remaining from colonial days, and inside is a moderately interesting museum of colonial paintings and furniture. It's worth a quick look inside to see what's left of the original building and its views of the Plaza and Avenida de Mayo. ⏱ *30 min. Bolívar 65 (at Rivadavia), Monserrat.* ☎ *11/ 4343-4387. Admission: AR$1 adults. Tues–Sat 10:30am–5pm; Sun 11:30am–6pm. Free tours Fri 3:30pm & Sat 2pm. Subte: Plaza de Mayo (A), Bolívar (E), or Catedral (D).*

❺ ★★ kids **Av. de Mayo.** This wide and graceful tree-lined avenue is the most historic thoroughfare in the city. Modeled after Paris's grand boulevards, it is a showcase of impressive office buildings, hotels, cafes, and theaters; a smorgasbord of Spanish, French, English, and Italian Belle Epoque and Art Nouveau influence. A highlight is **Casa de la Cultura,** the 1889 headquarters of the newspaper *La Prensa,* with its Versailles-like interior. Running beneath the avenue is the historic **A line** of the *subte,* or subway, the first built in South America; the Peru station, with its retro-style posters and kiosks, is the most authentic of the original 1913 stations. ⏱ *45 min. Av. de Mayo (between Perú & Sáenz Peña), Monserrat. Subte: Plaza de Mayo (A), Bolívar (E), or Catedral (D).*

❻ ★★★ **Café Tortoni.** The oldest, as well as most famous and atmospheric, cafe in Buenos Aires, little has changed at this institution since 1858 except for the attire of its patrons. Although it looks like a museum piece, with its rich woods, huge mirrors, ornate light fixtures, and stained-glass ceilings, it remains an essential gathering place for locals, as well as hordes of visitors. Politicians, artists, and intellectuals through the years, including Carlos Gardel (1890–1935), Jorge Luis Borges (1899–1986), and Federico García Lorca (1898–1936), have all held court at Tortoni. In the back is a cool theater hosting nightly tango performances. *Av. de Mayo 825.* ☎ *11/4342-4328. www. cafetortoni.com.ar. $$.*

The Avenido 9 de Julio is home to the Obelisco monument.

7 kids **Av. 9 de Julio/ Obelisco.** Whether or not it is in fact the widest street in the world, as Porteños love to tout Av. 9 de Julio, is a matter of dispute. Developed in 1937, and widened in the 1960s to its current 16 lanes, the avenue is home not only to some of the city's most important office buildings and a healthy share of its automobiles, but also to some lovingly landscaped garden areas. Four blocks to the north (at Corrientes), rising from the middle of the avenue, is the towering **Obelisco,** the symbol of Buenos Aires built in 1936 to commemorate the 400-year anniversary of the city's initial founding. Major national sporting events are frequently celebrated here, though one year, to mark International AIDS Day, the monument was draped with a giant condom. Another two blocks north is **Teatro Colón,** the renowned opera house that recently celebrated its 100-year-anniversary (but didn't open in time to celebrate after lengthy renovations). When again open, it's essential to visit for a concert or tour. ⏱ *20 min. Av. 9 de Julio (at Corrientes), Centro.*

Café Tortoni is the oldest and most famous café in Buenos Aires.

Subte: Carlos Pellegrini (B), Diagonal Norte (C), or 9 de Julio (D).

8 ★★★ kids **Palacio Barolo.** One of the most distinctive buildings in the city, this 22-story "palace" was the tallest in the city when completed in 1923. The Italian architect Mario Palanti built it for a local textile magnate and curiously styled the building to closely reflect aspects of Dante's *The Divine Comedy* (see p. 48). The lobby is gorgeous and the old-school elevators enchanting, but little prepares one for the breathtaking panoramic views from top floors. Tours are offered two days a week, but a visit to the tango clothing shop Tango Moda on the 16th floor also affords dramatic (free) views of the palace's cupola and all of Buenos Aires from two terraces. ⏱ *45 min. Av. de Mayo 1370 (at San José), Centro.* ☎ *11/4383-1065 (15/5027-9035 for tour information). www.pbarolo.com. ar. Admission: AR$15 adults. Tours Mon & Thurs on the hr. 2–7pm; English & Spanish. Subte: Sáenz Peña (A).*

9 ★★ **Palacio del Congreso.** At the end of Av. de Mayo, forming a bookend with the Casa Rosada, is the imposing Greco-Roman Congress building, constructed in 1909 of gray granite and topped by a greenish copper dome. Tours of the Congress's opulent interior take visitors to the Salón Rosado, now renamed for Eva Perón, who christened the room as a place that women, newly granted the right to vote, could discuss issues without the interference of men (Evita lay in state at Congreso for 2 weeks of public viewing after her death in 1952). ⏱ *1 hr. Yrigoyen 1849, Centro.* ☎ *11/4370-7100 or 11/6310-7100, ext. 3725. Free guided tours in English on Mon, Tues, Thurs, & Fri 11am & 4pm; in Spanish Mon, Tues, Thurs, & Fri 11am, 4pm, & 5pm. Subte: Congreso (A).*

Plaza San Martin is one of the city's favorite parks.

10 ★★★ kids **A Line Subte.** A great way to experience the still-running, antique subway is to hop aboard the A line back from Congreso. You can ride it all the way to Plaza de Mayo, although Estación Peru retains the most period charm, with turn-of-the-20th-century posters and charmingly old-school kiosks, tiles, and lamps transporting commuters back in time. The original wood-paneled cars, introduced in 1913 as part of the first subway system in South America, still run the line, even though some newer cars have been introduced; if you're riding as much for the experience as the transport, wait for one of the older cars. ⏱ *20 min. From Congreso to Plaza de Mayo, Peru station, Av. de Mayo 500, Monserrat. www.subte.com.ar. Admission AR$0.90 adults.*

11 ★★ kids **Plaza San Martín.** This handsome park in the Retiro district is one of Buenos Aires's treasured green spaces. Palm trees, *palos borrachos*, and (in spring) the abundant lavender flowers of *jacarandás* frame views of an imposing skyscraper, the 1935 Edificio Kavanagh, and two stunning early 20th-century aristocratic mansions: the **Palacio San Martín** (former home to the Argentine Foreign Service), and **Palacio Paz,** a massive and extraordinary palace reminiscent of Versailles, with a miniature gilded opera house within and one wing housing the Círculo Militar, a weapons and military museum. 🕐 *30 min. (90 min if touring Círculo Militar). Palacio Paz: Av. Santa Fe 750 (at Maipú), Retiro.* ☎ *11/4311-1071. www.circulomilitar.org. Admission: AR$15 adults. Círculo Militar tours in Spanish Tues & Fri 11am & 3pm, Wed & Thurs 11am & 4pm, Sat 11am; English Tues & Thurs 3:30pm. Subte: San Martín (C).*

⓬ **Calle Florida.** A pedestrian-only street that was once Buenos Aires's most glamorous is today its most commercial. Its swank buildings, somewhat difficult to appreciate amid the hubbub, attest to Florida's erstwhile elegance and status as the city's most famous shopping promenade. Some of that, ironically, is still on view within **Galerías Pacífico** (no. 737), a shopping mall with real pedigree; it's even a National Historic Monument. The 1891 building is enlivened by a central dome with colorful, expressive frescoes painted by five Argentine muralists in the 1940s. Other exquisite buildings on Calle Florida include Centro Naval (no. 801); Galería Guemes (no. 165), drab on the outside but with a gorgeously restored back entrance on San Martín 170 and glorious glass dome; and Bank of Boston (no. 99). 🕐 *45 min. Florida (between Av. Alvear & Av. Corrientes), Centro. Subte: Florida (B) or San Martín (C).*

⓭ ★ **Florida Garden.** A classic cafe from the days when Calle Florida reeked of elegance and everyone from politicians and bankers to student activists and artists gathered here. It's still a revered spot for coffee, chocolate cake, sandwiches (including the house specialty, *pebete de pan negro*—ham and cheese on house-baked brown bread), and in the bar at the back, a stiff drink at the end of the day. *Florida 899.* ☎ *11/4312-7902. Daily 6:30am–midnight. $$.*

The Galerias Pacifico shopping mall is a National Historic Monument.

The Best in **Two Days**

(i)	Information
(M)	Metro Stop
▪	Point of Interest
✉	Post Office

1. Fundación Proa
2. La Perla
3. Caminito
4. Port/Puente Transbordador
5. Plaza Dorrego
6. Casa de los Ezeiza
7. Colección de Arte Fortabat
8. Basílica Nuestra Señora del Pilar
9. Cementerio de la Recoleta
10. Avenida Alvear
11. La Biela

On day two, we move south of the center to two historic neighborhoods, La Boca and San Telmo—where tango was born, nurtured, and lives on—followed by a glimpse of forward-looking Buenos Aires in Puerto Madero. And we finish in rarified Recoleta, home to some of Buenos Aires's finest apartment buildings, hotels, and shops, and the stunning cemetery where Evita and other pillars of Argentine society are buried. START: **Taxi to Vuelta de Rocha (La Boca).**

1 ★★ **Fundación Proa.** Standing in stark, gleaming white contrast to colorful Caminito is this contemporary art museum and foundation, one of the city's most interesting and progressive art spaces. In addition to excellent exhibits (in past years, featuring Marcel Duchamp, Jenny Holzer, Sol LeWitt, and Sebastião Salgado), the recently transformed building—an ingeniously converted Italianate mansion with a modern glass addition and nod to the area's edgy past—contains a cafe, library, wide terrace with great views of the port and barrio, and auditorium holding occasional concerts and film series. ⏱ *1 hr. Av. Pedro de Mendoza 1929, La Boca.* ☎ *11/4104-1000. www.proa.org. Admission: AR $10 adults, AR$6 students, AR$3 seniors. Tues–Sun 11am–8pm. Subte: No access.*

2 ★★★ **La Perla.** This 1920 cantina—said to have been a brothel in years past—is about as cinematic a cafe as you'll find in Buenos Aires, chock full of worn wooden tables, walls covered in old photographs, mirrors, and local artwork, and colorful seltzer bottles on the tables. Protected by law as a cafe notable, the bar has long been a hangout of the artistic and politically motivated set, though today its prices are more likely to appeal to foreigners. Grab a seat by one of the windows for a great view of the port and touristy goings-on at the start of Caminito. *Av. Pedro de Mendoza 1899.* ☎ *11/4301-2985. $$.*

La Perla.

The pedestrian-only alleyway of Caminito is a magnet for tourists.

3 ★ kids **Caminito.** Sure, it's one of the most touristy and colorful spots in the city, but the pedestrian-only alleyway—full of wood-and-corrugated-tin tenement houses with rickety balconies that used to house new immigrants—is so brightly painted and perfect for pictures with tango dancers and street performers that you can't very well skip it completely. **La Boca,** the old port area, is where Italian immigrants who worked the shipyards settled, and locals claim the tango was born among the working-class (and sailors and prostitutes) in the late 19th century. Part of one of the city's oldest residential neighborhoods, the local artist Benito Quinquela Martín (1890–1977) conceived of the street in 1959 as a way to give other local artists a massive outdoor canvas outlet and to feel proud about their rundown barrio. While it hasn't transformed the district—just venture a couple streets off Caminito to see the plain brown reality of La Boca—it has converted it into a tourist magnet. ⏲ *30 min. Av. Pedro de Mendoza (at Vuelta de Rocha), La Boca. Subte: No access.*

4 **Port/Puente Transbordador.** Buenos Aires was founded near La Boca for the first time in 1536 (though the settlement was soon abandoned), and not for nothing are the city's residents called Porteños (people of the port). Today the port, though, is anything but picturesque—in fact, it's downright malodorous—but it's a crucial part of the city, given its past maritime and commercial importance. That significance is perhaps best symbolized by the 1914 iron transporter bridge that carried trains and cargo across the Riochuela (canal) until the mid-20th century. ⏲ *15 min. Av. Pedro de Mendoza (at Almirante Brown), La Boca. Subte: No access.*

5 ★★★ kids **Plaza Dorrego.** The heart of historic, bohemian San Telmo is this laid-back plaza with a smattering of bars, cafes, and restaurants. On Sundays, however, the renowned San Telmo Antiques Fair takes over it and the surrounding streets, transforming the square into the shopping and tourist epicenter of Buenos Aires. Sellers and shoppers crowd the plaza, the

The port is a critical part of the history of Buenos Aires.

San Telmo never fails to entertain.

second-oldest in the city, while tango dancers and orchestras fight for space on the packed streets leading to it. It's worth planning your trip to Argentina to include a Sunday morning in San Telmo; whether it's people-watching or serious silver and glass antiques you're interested in, this busy square cannot fail to entertain. And be sure to check out the superb permanent antiques dealers and art galleries on the cobblestoned streets radiating out from the plaza (principally along Humberto I and Defensa). ⏱ *1 hr. Defensa (at Humberto I), San Telmo. Subte: Independencia (C).*

⑥ ★ **Casa de los Ezeiza.** Few places so succinctly sum up San Telmo's past and present. This sprawling, Spanish-style mansion was constructed in 1850, just before yellow fever would drive wealthy local residents to (literally) higher ground in Recoleta. It later became a *conventillo,* or tenement house occupied by several families, and then a school and warehouse before its current function housing antiques dealers and assorted shops. With its two interior patios, faded walls, and worn black-and-white tiled flooring, the house is a shadow of its former grandeur and looks a bit like a multifamily dwelling in Havana, but it

The Real Caminito

Caminito ("little alley") was inspired by the classic tango of the same name, not the other way around. The famous tango *Caminito,* by Juan de Dios Filiberto (1885–1964) and Gabino Coria Peñaloza (1881–1975), might appear to be an homage to the little street in La Boca, but in fact, the song dates to 1926 and has nothing at all to do with it, La Boca, or even Buenos Aires: Rather, it speaks nostalgically of a flower-bedecked path in Argentina's far-off La Rioja province.

seems perfect for today's bohemian and antiques-crazed San Telmo. ⊕ *20 min. Defensa 1179, San Telmo. Subte: Independencia (C).*

7 ★★ **Colección de Arte Fortabat.** The nearby district of Puerto Madero, the site of recycled 19th-century warehouses and the city's most rampant new development, is also home to its newest art museum, garnering a great deal of attention for its avant-garde design by Rafael Viñoly. In spectacular style, it houses the art collection—including some of the biggest names among both Argentine and international artists of the last 100 years—of one of Argentina's richest women, Amalia Lacroze de Fortabat. Inaugurated in November 2008, the cylindrical building features fantastic views of Puerto Madero, the yacht club, and the city beyond from the upstairs galleries. Previously best known for its office buildings and upscale restaurants, Puerto Madero is a good place to grab lunch alongside politicians and business folks. ⊕ *1 hr. Olga Cossettini 141, Puerto Madero.* ☎ *11/4310-6600. www.coleccionfortabat.org.ar. Admission: AR$15 adults, AR$7 students & seniors. Tues–Fri noon–9pm; Sat–Sun 10am–9pm. Subte: L.N. Alem (B).*

8 ★★ **Basílica Nuestra Señora del Pilar.** The Recoleta neighborhood may not be as old as San Telmo or La Boca, but it does have the second-oldest church in Buenos Aires, which was originally part of a convent belonging to the Padres Recoletos. This attractive church, inaugurated in 1732, has an unadorned colonial exterior, though its current pristine whiteness is a modern alteration (in colonial days, it was white and sun-yellow). Inside, you'll find outstanding Spanish colonial artwork and a baroque, silver-plated altar brought from Alto Perú.

The Basílica Nuestra Señora del Pilar is the city's second-oldest church.

The small religious art museum within the old convent is worth a visit to see the original flooring, windows, and other period details where cloistered nuns once lived. ⊕ *30 min. Junín 1904, Recoleta.* ☎ *11/4803-6793. Admission: AR$3 adults. Tues–Sat 10:30am–6:15pm; Sun 2:30–6:15pm. Subte: No access.*

9 ★★★ kids **Cementerio de la Recoleta.** One of the most famous cemeteries in the world, and not just because Evita is buried here, this moving and beautiful city of the dead is one of the highlights of Buenos Aires. Many of the tombs and mausoleums of Argentina's wealthiest and most powerful residents are audacious, no-expense-spared works of Art Nouveau, Gothic, and neo-Classical art: small marble and granite houses with soaring angels and crosses gracing tree-lined boulevards. Opened in 1822, Recoleta is even more exclusive than the neighborhood that has grown up around it: the final resting place of military generals, presidents, and aristocrats, including Bartolomé Mitre (1821–1906), the first president of

Argentina; José Paz (1842–1912), the founder of *La Prensa*; and, of course, Eva Perón, buried in a relatively modest mausoleum indicated by her father's surname, Família Duarte. 🕐 *1 hr. Junín 1790 (at Plaza Francesa), Recoleta.* ☎ *11/4804-7040. Free admission. Free English-language tours Tues & Thurs 11am. Subte: No access.*

🔟 ★ **Avenida Alvear.** Recoleta drips with glamour and wealth, something one can get a taste of by strolling along this swank residential and commercial avenue. Home to elegant apartment buildings and two of the city's most famous and elite hotels, the Alvear Palace (no. 1883) and Park Hyatt/Palacio Duhau (no. 1661), it is also the site of luxurious digs for high-end fashion stores, including Hermés (no. 1981), Valentino (no. 1923), Ralph Lauren (no. 1780), and Emporio Armani (no. 1750), as well as shops with local

flavor, such as the exquisite silversmith Juan Carlos Pallarols (no. 1883). 🕐 *45 min. Av. Alvear (between Schiaffino & Montevideo), Recoleta. Subte: No access.*

☕ ★★ **La Biela.** One of the city's most famous and pedigreed cafes, with a history that goes back to the mid-19th century, La Biela is where Recoleta's elite come to sip coffee and nibble on petit-fours on the broad terrace, under umbrellas and massive ombú branches. It's a classic, European-style cafe inside, where the Argentine author Julio Cortázar (1914–1984) and other illustrious figures settled in over the years, but outdoors is where the practiced art of people-watching, second only to polo season among this crowd, goes on. *Quintana 600.* ☎ *11/4804-4135. www.labiela.com. $$$.*

Cafe La Biela is a great place for sipping coffee and people-watching.

The Best in **Three Days**

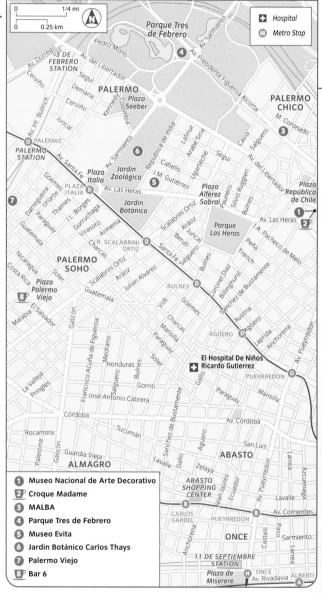

0 1/4 mi
0 0.25 km

Parque Tres de Febrero

Hospital
M Metro Stop

1. Museo Nacional de Arte Decorativo
2. Croque Madame
3. MALBA
4. Parque Tres de Febrero
5. Museo Evita
6. Jardín Botánico Carlos Thays
7. Palermo Viejo
8. Bar 6

Moving northwest for a more relaxed third day, we visit **Palermo**, a sprawling neighborhood of upscale apartment buildings, expansive parks and gardens, and several of the city's most interesting museums. Palermo Viejo, a formerly rundown area, has become the city's hottest zone for restaurants, boutique shops, and chic little hotels—and its cobblestoned streets and chic venues are perfect for an afternoon of window shopping. START: **Taxi to Av. Libertador (at Pereyra Lucena).**

1 ★★ **Museo Nacional de Arte Decorativo.** Calling this the "National Museum of Decorative Arts" does it a bit of a disservice, since it is in fact an extraordinary private residence with a tremendous art collection, and the only early-20th-century French-styled mansion in Buenos Aires open to the public. The **Palacio Errázuriz** itself is as rich in architectural detail as the collection of 4,000 Euro-centric "decorative arts" objects it holds, donated to the state by the family—Chilean diplomat Matías Errázuriz and his wife, Josefina de Alvear, who possessed one of the city's great fortunes in the early 20th century—in 1937. The massive home was designed in 1911 by the French architect René Sergent (1865–1927), also responsible for

the building that houses the current U.S. embassy. The English Tudor two-story Grand Hall, with its massive fireplace, is extraordinary, as is the Louis XV–style dining room. The art collection includes works by El Greco (c. 1541–1614) and Manet (1832–1883), as well as 17th- and 18th-century Flemish tapestries. 🕐 *1 hr. Av. del Libertador 1902, Palermo.* ☎ *11/4801-8248. www.mnad. org. Admission: AR$2 adults, AR$1 students; free on Tues. Tues–Sun 2–7pm. Guided visits in English Tues–Sat 2:30pm. Subte: No access.*

2 ★ **Croque Madame.** Just inside the massive gate to the Museo Nacional de Arte Decorativo is this charming, and surprisingly elegant, cafe-restaurant, in a sweet little

The Museo Nacional de Arte Decorativo houses a tremendous art collection.

house with a sweeping staircase, chandeliers, and relaxing outdoor terrace. It's the perfect spot for a late breakfast or full tea service, but the very complete menu—with pizzas, salads, namesake croque madames and croque monsiuers, risottos, and even fish dishes—makes it a great stop for lunch or dinner, too. *Av. del Libertador 1902.* ☎ *11/ 4806-8639. $$.*

❸ ★★ **MALBA.** The Museo de Arte Latinoamericano de Buenos Aires, occupying a dramatic modern stone-and-glass building, is in fact the private contemporary art collection of Eduardo Costantini, a local businessman. Major Latin American artists are represented, including Diego Rivera (1886–1957), Frida Kahlo (1907–1954), Roberto Matta (1911–2002), and Wilfredo Lam (1902–1982), as well as top Argentine painters such as Antonio Berni (1905–1981) and Xul Solar (1887–1963). In addition to the estimable collection, the building is distinguished by its abundant natural light, a two-storey central atrium, and a terrific cafe-restaurant (Café des Arts; ☎ 11/4808-0754) with a pretty outdoor terrace, a favorite

lunch spot of many professionals who work in the area. ⏱ *1 hr. Av. Figueroa Alcorta 3415, Palermo Chico.* ☎ *11/4808-6500. www. malba.org.ar. Admission: AR$15 adults, free for students & seniors; free admission on Wed. Thurs–Mon noon–8pm; Wed noon–9pm. Subte: No access.*

❹ ★★ **kids** **Parque Tres de Febrero.** Buenos Aires's answer to New York's Central Park is the city's most prized green space, often called the "Woods of Palermo" by locals. The sprawling park, decreed by President Sarmiento in 1872, features over 1,000 acres of gardens, three lakes, walking paths, and woods. It's the city's lungs, the place Porteños hit on weekends to run, bicycle, go inline skating, rent paddle boats, sunbathe, and stroll. Don't miss El Rosedal, a lovely rose garden with more than 12,000 plantings, designed by the Frenchman Carlos Thays (1839–1934), responsible for the landscaping on Av. 9 de Julio and other parks in the city; or the immense statue Monumento a los Españoles, a gift from the Spanish government in 1910 (Av. Libertador at Av. Sarmiento). ⏱ *1 hr. Av. Libertador (between Av.*

You'll find major Latin American artists at MALBA.

The Museo Evita helps explain the pivotal figure's iconic status.

Casares & Av. Dorrego), Palermo. Subte: Plaza Italia (D).

5 ★★ kids **Museo Evita.** Eva Perón became a surprisingly pivotal, and lasting, figure in Argentine life for someone who was the wife of the president and died at the young age of 33. This intimate museum dedicated to her life—in a lovely Renaissance-style residence on a quiet Palermo street, which Perón herself appropriated and transformed into a shelter for women and children— goes a good way towards explaining the enduring fascination with Evita. Adored by throngs of Argentine workers and women, her remains took a long and convoluted way to reach their current resting place in Recoleta Cemetery, a tale of intrigue and caper, retold in a short film on Evita's life. Through it and other exhibits, including remarkably preserved dresses, jewelry, and personal belongings, the museum explains the reasons underlying Evita's iconic status, reminding us of her work in health care, getting women the right to vote, facilitating access to education for marginalized millions, and increasing wages for union workers. More than a half-century after her death, she continues to divide Argentines, still largely along class lines. The attached restaurant-cafe (J.M. Gutiérrez 3926; ☎ 11/4800-1599) has a beautiful, verdant outdoor terrace and is an excellent stop for breakfast, lunch, or dinner—or just tea or a cocktail. ⏲ 1 hr. Lafinur 2988 (at J.M. Gutiérrez), Palermo. ☎ 11/4807-0306. www.evitaperon.org. Admission: AR$12 adults. Nov–Apr Tues–Sun 11am–7pm; May–Oct Tues–Sun 1–7pm. Subte: Plaza Italia (D).

6 ★ kids **Jardín Botánico Carlos Thays.** Also conceived by the landscape designer Carlos Thays in 1898, and named in his honor, the botanical garden is a delightful refuge from the city. Although in recent years it became abandoned and overrun by a population of feral cats, it has been slowly nursed back to health and is again a lovely place to stroll amid indigenous flora, massive trees, and cacti, as well as fountains, statuary, and a charming wrought-iron greenhouse. ⏲ 30 min. Av. Santa Fe 3951, Palermo. ☎ 11/4831-4527. www.jardinbotanico. gov.ar. Free admission. Nov–Mar 8am–8pm; Apr–Oct 9am–6pm. Subte: Plaza Italia (D).

The botanical garden is a delightful refuge from the city.

Modern Bar 6 boasts excellent cocktails, DJs, and free WiFi.

7 ★★ **Palermo Viejo.** A formerly forgotten area of rundown, squat buildings, this neighborhood has gotten a makeover in the last few years, and now it's Buenos Aires's coolest barrio, where the chicest boutique hotels, shops, restaurants, and hipster bars have taken root. While the concentration of places to spend your pesos is daunting and the residential towers have moved in with a vengeance, the area hasn't lost its charm. On a late afternoon, it's a joy to wander the cobblestoned streets and small alleyways, and take in the shops, many of which are so chic and visually creative that they practically dare you not to step in. Whether you're shopping for one-of-a-kind handbags and shoes, sheepskin rugs, silver-and-horn trays, or uber-trendy clothes, you'll find it here. The epicenter of life in Palermo Viejo is Plaza Serrano (also called Plaza Cortázar); look for the quiet *pasajes* (alleyways) Soria, Russel, and Santa Rosa. Cool cafes, restaurants, and hotels abound. 🕐 *2 hrs. Bordered by Av. Corrientes, Av. Scalabrini Ortiz, Av. Santa Fe, & Av. Dorrego. Subte: No access.*

8 ★ **Bar 6.** A modern, but relaxed, high-ceilinged space with cement floors, couches, and comfortable sitting chairs, this restaurant is perfect for a leisurely coffee or great fruit batido (shake), as well as sandwiches, quesadillas, and more ambitious fare such as ceviche and grilled lamb. Plenty of folks come early for breakfast and others late for the excellent cocktails, DJs, and free Wi-Fi. *Armenia 1676.* ☎ *11/4833-6807. www.barseis.com. $$.* ●

Palermo Cómo?

As Palermo Viejo has grown in popularity and become the center of all things hip, it has been unofficially subdivided, somewhat annoyingly, into districts known as Palermo Soho, Palermo Hollywood, and even Palermo Queens—signaling that Porteños, despite their city having been lauded as the hippest spot in South America, still look beyond their borders for inspiration.

Historic Buenos Aires

1. Museo Histórico Nacional
2. Plaza Dorrego
3. Nuestra Señora de Belén
4. El Zanjón
5. Bar El Federal
6. Plaza de Mayo
7. Librería de Ávila
8. Farmacia La Estrella
9. Manzana de las Luces
10. Avenida de Mayo
11. Basílica Nuestra Señora del Pilar
12. Cementerio de la Recoleta
13. Alvear Palace Hotel Bar

Previous Page: Signs of Porteños love of fútbol are everywhere in the city.

Deep historical roots lie just beneath the surface of modern Buenos Aires. This tour delves into San Telmo, where the city was first settled, and Monserrat, the historic quarter and site of the city's second (and lasting) founding in 1580, as well as the pivotal events that jump-started the May Revolution in 1810 and the road toward independence. Finish in Recoleta, where aristocratic families fled after the yellow-fever epidemic wiped out much of the neighborhood in the late 19th century. START: **Taxi to Parque Lezama (San Telmo) or subte to Constitución (C).**

1 ★ Museo Histórico Nacional. Begin tracing the city's history with a visit to the former colonial mansion of the Lezama family, today site of the National History Museum, which addresses Argentine history from the 16th through the 20th centuries. On display are items recovered from Jesuit missions and items instrumental in the War of Independence against Spain, including the first Argentine flag, flown in 1813. Among the highlights is the bedroom of General José de San Martín (1778–1850), brought here from his last home and reconstructed. Lezama Park is said to be the spot where Pedro de Mendoza (c. 1487–1537) first settled in 1536, as well as the headquarters of the Company of Guinea's slave operations in the 18th century. ⏱ *30 min. Defensa 1600 (Parque Lezama), San Telmo.* ☎ *11/4307-4457. Free admission. Tues–Sun noon–6pm. Closed Jan. Subte: Constitución (C).*

This 200-year-old church took 70 years to complete.

2 ★★★ kids Plaza Dorrego. The second-oldest square in the city, and a National Historic Monument, Plaza Dorrego is where Porteños formally declared their independence from Spain in 1816. A market square in the second half of the 19th century, since 1970, it has been the site of a lively antiques fair every Sunday, with high-quality 19th-century silver and glass pieces among the offerings. Other days, visit some of the superb antiques stores (such as Gil Antiguedades and Cándido Silva) dealing in colonial religious art, chandeliers, and 18th- and 19th-century furniture and silver along the cobblestoned streets Humberto I and Defensa, and peek into **Casa de los Ezeiza** (Defensa 1179), an 1850 Spanish-style mansion that later became a *conventillo,* or tenement house, occupied by several families after yellow fever swept the district. ⏱ *1 hr. See bullet 5, p 16.*

Underground tunnels that run beneath the city were built in the 18th century.

3 ★ **Nuestra Señora de Belén.** Begun in 1735 by the Jesuit architect who also built the old town hall on Plaza de Mayo, this church (also confusingly called San Pedro Telmo) retains colonial elements, even though it took some 7 decades to complete. In 1767, the Bethlemites (an extinct English order of monks) took it over. The organ and oil paintings are from the 18th century, while the impressive pulpit dates from 1805. ⏱ *20 min. Humberto I 340.* ☎ *11/4361-1168. Subte: Independencia (C).*

4 ★★ kids **El Zanjón.** Underground tunnels once ran beneath much of Buenos Aires, and when this 1830 residence, in ruins, was being restored, workers discovered a massive cistern that led them to extensive passageways where water was channeled from the river. What was to become a restaurant was transformed into an archaeological dig. Excavations revealed that the house was built on top of foundations that date to Buenos Aires's official founding in 1580, and the underground tunnels were part of a labyrinth said to have once reached as far as where Av. 9 de Julio is currently. It is thought that the tunnels were built starting in 1730 and then sealed by the late 19th century. They and the house have been meticulously restored, and sections of original foundations and brick vaults, as well as tools and ceramics, are handsomely lighted and displayed. ⏱ *1 hr. Defensa 755, San Telmo.* ☎ *11/4361-3002. www.elzanjon.com.ar. Mon–Fri 11am–2pm; Sun 1–6pm. Mon–Fri 1-hr. tours on the hr., AR$36 adults; Sun 30-min tours (required) every ½-hr., AR$15 adults. Subte: Independencia (C).*

5 ★★★ **Bar El Federal.** A law-protected bar notable, this 1864 cafe-restaurant—a former grocer with a long, original wood-carved bar and antique cash registers—resonates with history and makes a great stop for coffee or a good lunch—or perhaps a wee-hours meal and drink if you're stumbling out of a club or tango show in the neighborhood. *Carlos Calvo 599.* ☎ *11/4300-4313. $.*

6 ★★ **Plaza de Mayo.** The heart of the *casco histórico,* the oldest square in Buenos Aires, was established in 1580, the date of the city's second founding. It was the site of the 1810 May Revolution, which led to Argentina's independence; the **Pirámide de Mayo** in its center commemorating that event was the first monument built in the city, in 1811. At the east end is the **Casa Rosada,** which dates to 1884; at the other end, on the north side, is the **Catedral Metropolitana,** completed in 1882 after nearly 150 years of work (the city's first cathedral occupied the same spot in 1622). Inside the Cathedral is the tomb of General San Martín, the "Father of the Nation," whose remains were moved here in 1880. Across the street is the **Cabildo,** the old town hall, on the spot where the town council met beginning at the end of the 16th century, and the only public building on Plaza de Mayo remaining from colonial days. ⏱ *45 min. See bullet* **2***, p 9.*

7 **Librería de Ávila.** The first bookstore in Buenos Aires, dating from 1785 (when it was called Librería del Colegio), was a companion to the university, and more than 2 centuries later, it remains in operation, with current and rare titles available and a downstairs literary cafe. ⏱ *15 min. Alsina 500, Monserrat.* ☎ *11/4331-8989. Mon–Sun 9am–6pm. Subte: Perú (A) or Bolívar (E).*

8 ★ **Farmacia La Estrella.** This historic pharmacy, still dispensing antibiotics and toothpaste today, dates to 1834. By today's standards, it's surprisingly grand, with carved mahogany columns, Carrara marble, Murano glass, and allegorical ceiling murals depicting health and medicine. Above the pharmacy is the idiosyncratic **Museo de la Ciudad,** with quirky quotidian objects, such as toys, documenting the history of Buenos Aires. ⏱ *30 min. Defensa 201/219 (at Alsina), Monserrat.* ☎ *11/4343-4040 or 11/4331-9855. Museum admission: AR$1 adults; free Mon & Wed. Mon–Fri 11am–7pm; Sun 3–7pm. Subte: Bolívar (E).*

The wood-carved bar at Bar El Federal is part of the original 1864 construction.

The Avenido de Mayo is lined with Belle Epoque architecture.

9 ★★ **Manzana de las Luces.** On this historic "Block of Enlightenment," the oldest collection of buildings in Buenos Aires and the intellectual heart of the city, the Jesuits settled in 1633 and remained until their expulsion from Argentina in 1767. Underground tunnels from the 18th century (which may have had a military purpose or been used in contraband) run beneath the block. In 1686, the Jesuits lay the foundations for **Iglesia de San Ignacio** (Bolívar 225), the oldest existing church in Buenos Aires. ⏱ *45 min. Perú 272 (at Moreno), Monserrat.* ☎ *11/4342-6973 for tours. www.manzanadelasluces.gov.ar. Admission: AR $6–AR$7 adults. Guided visits (including tunnels) Mon 1 & 3pm; Tues–Fri 3pm; Sat–Sun 3, 4:30, & 6pm. Subte: Bolívar (E).*

10 ★★★ **Avenida de Mayo.** This grand, European-style boulevard, inaugurated in 1894, is the most historic in the city, lined with Belle Epoque architecture. The axis of Argentine political power, connecting the Casa Rosada (House of Government) to Congreso (the seat of Congress), it is most representative of the city's Golden Age. By 1910, 18 hotels had been erected here, along with the city's most popular cafes and theaters. ⏱ *2 hrs.; Av. de Mayo & Bolívar. Subte: Perí (A).*

11 ★★ **Basílica Nuestra Señora del Pilar.** Recoleta grew up around this colonial church, the second-oldest in Buenos Aires, that harkens back to 1716, when it was part of a convent belonging to French Recoletos (Franciscan) monks. Inside, you'll find Spanish colonial artwork and a baroque, silver-plated altar brought from Alto Perú. The old convent houses a religious art museum with original flooring, windows and other period details. ⏱ *30 min. See bullet **8**, p 18.*

12 ★★★ **kids** **Cementerio de la Recoleta.** Opened in 1822, this stunning necropolis—Buenos Aires's first public cemetery—is the final resting place of military generals, presidents, and aristocrats, including Bartolomé Mitre (1821–1906), the first president of Argentina; José Paz (1842–1912), the founder of *La Prensa;* and, of course, Eva Perón (1919–1952), buried in 1976 (after her remains were finally recovered, in 1971, after being missing for 16 years) in a mausoleum indicated by her father's surname, Familia Duarte. ⏱ *1 hr. See bullet **9**, p 18.*

The Basílica Nuestra Señora del Pilar was built in 1716.

Avenida de Mayo

The 1889 headquarters of the national newspaper *La Prensa*, **A** **Casa de la Cultura,** contains a room that is a copy of a Versailles palace salon. Buenos Aires's subway, opened in 1913, was South America's first, and the original wooden cars of **B** **★★★ Subte Línea A** still run beneath Av. de Mayo; **C** **★★ Estación Peru** has been returned to its former glory, with retro advertising posters and original red-and-cream-colored kiosks, tiles, and lamps. Buenos Aires's oldest cafe, **D** **★★★ Café Tortoni**—in continuous operation since 1858—was a hangout for Carlos Gardel (1890–1935), Jorge Luis Borges (1899–1986), and the Spanish poet Federico García

Lorca (1898–1936). García Lorca spent most of the year he lived in Buenos Aires (in 1933 and 1934) at **E** **Hotel Castelar,** a stately 1929 hotel. Lorca also frequented **F** **★★ Los 36 Billares,** an 1894 institution that was the first cafe in the city to feature billiards tables (still popular, downstairs). **G** **★★ Congreso's** construction in 1909 meant the demolition of several then-new grand apartment buildings. **H** **Confiteria del Molino,** a long-revered 1915 cafe, went belly up in the mid-1990s and sits in the shadow of Congress like a decrepit reminder of the failures of the public servants next door.

13 **★★ Alvear Palace Hotel Bar.** Within this standard-bearer for luxury hotels in Buenos Aires, inaugurated in 1932, is a rich, Old World bar that's the perfect place for a cocktail after visiting the city's most historic sights. *Av. Alvear 1883.* ☎ *11/4808-2100.* **$$$.**

Where Else But Buenos Aires?

1 La Bombonera/Museo de la Pasión Boquense
2 Torre de los Ingleses/ Monumento a los Caidos en Malvinas
3 Galerías Pacífico
4 Madres de la Plaza de Mayo
5 Casa Rosada
6 El General

7 Confitería La Ideal
8 Cementerio de Recoleta
9 El Ateneo Grand Splendid
10 Museo Evita
11 Hipódromo de Palermo/ Campo Argentino de Polo
12 Heladeria Sarpiecco
13 Carritos de la Costanera Sur

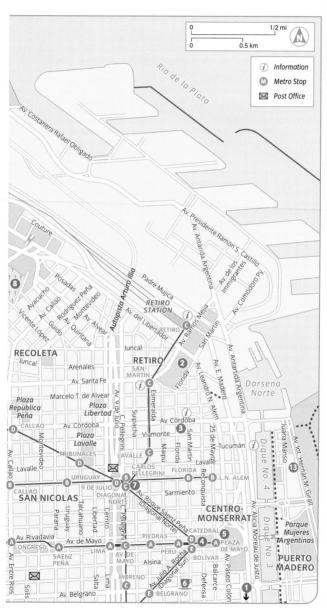

This tour explores what makes Buenos Aires unique, quite apart from the mega-wide Av. 9 de Julio and the touristy Caminito promenade: From *fútbol* and polo horses to a personal museum about Evita and the Malvinas controversy, these are places where you'll get a real taste of the Argentine people and their capital city (for tango, another indelible feature of Buenos Aires, turn to the next tour). START: **Taxi to La Bombonera (La Boca).**

① ★★ kids La Bombonera/ Museo de la Pasión Boquense. Argentina perennially ranks as one of the elite national *fútbol*, or soccer, programs in the world, and Boca Juniors—one-time home to Diego Maradona—is one of its most famous teams. Boca's blue-and-yellow-clad followers put the fan in fanatic. If you can catch a match at the massive 1940 stadium Estadio Club Boca Juniors—better known as La Bombonera—preferably against crosstown rival River Plate, it is likely to be the highlight of your trip. The museum in the basement of the stadium is a walk through Boca Juniors history and paraphernalia, especially fun for soccer-playing kids, followed by a visit to the cavernous stadium. ⏱ *1 hr. Brandsen 805, La Boca.* ☎ *11/4362-1100. www. museoboquense.com. Admission: AR$20–$AR30 adults. Daily 10am–7pm. Subte: No access.*

② Torre de los Ingleses/Monumento a los Caídos en Malvinas. Argentina's answer to Big Ben, this clock tower was a gift from British immigrants to commemorate the centennial of the 1810 May Revolution. (Take the elevator to the top of the tower for panoramic views of Retiro and sights as far away as Puerto Madero.) But the English Tower has been joined by a monument that reflects something quite different about Argentina's relationship with the English. Placed deliberately across the street, the somber Monument to the Fallen in the Malvinas pays tribute to the Argentine casualties suffered at the hands of the British in the 1982 Malvinas/Falkland Islands War. The monument—with names etched in black marble much like at the Vietnam Memorial in Washington, D.C.—and its strategic location ensure that Argentines

Boca Juniors is one of Argentina's most famous fútbol teams.

The Monument to the Fallen pays tribute to those who died in the Falkland Islands War.

won't soon forget the conflict. ⏱ *30 min. Torre: Av. Libertador 49, Retiro.* ☎ *11/ 4311-0186. Free admission. Mon–Fri 10am–5pm; Sat–Sun 10am–6:30pm. Subte: Retiro. Malvinas Memorial: Av. Libertador/Plaza San Martín. Subte: San Martín (C) or Retiro (C).*

③ ★ kids Galerías Pacífico. This 1891 shopping mall along pedestrian-only **Calle Florida,** once the epitome of glamour in the Argentine capital, is a formidable reminder of Buenos Aires's early-20th-century wealth. The central dome of the 19th-century building is painted with several eye-catching frescoes—a series depicting the history of mankind, painted in 1945 by five well-known Argentine artists, including Antonio Berni (1905–1981). ⏱ *45 min. Florida (at Córdoba), Centro.* ☎ *11/5555-5110. www.galerias pacifico.com.ar. Subte: Florida (B) or San Martín (C).*

④ ★★★ Madres de la Plaza de Mayo. Argentina's famed Mothers of the Plaza de Mayo staged one of the most moving political protests of the last century—at first silently gathering, and then forcefully appealing to the military and successive democratic governments to investigate and take responsibility for the disappearances of their children and husbands. Their families were abducted—and for some, tortured and murdered—by the military juntas of the 1970s and early 1980s,

during the regimes' "Dirty War" on its citizens. The courageous, determined mothers don't gather religiously as they once did every Thursday afternoon in the Plaza de Mayo, wearing their trademark white headscarves bearing the names of loved ones, but their presence is still very much a part of Argentine politics. Estimates of the missing still unaccounted for range from 10,000 to 30,000; for many families, this gruesome chapter of Argentine history still has not been closed. ⏱ *1 hr. Av. de Mayo (at Bolívar), Monserrat. www.madres.org. Subte: Plaza de Mayo (A), Bolívar (E), or Catedral (D).*

⑤ ★ Casa Rosada. Argentina's unique "Pink House," the presidential palace, is where Evita Perón gave her famous discourse to her beloved supporters (immortalized

The Mothers of the Plaza de Mayo still gather weekly to protest lost family members.

as "Don't Cry for Me, Argentina!" in the Broadway play), and in the late '90s, President Ménem allowed the filmmaker Alan Parker to stage his shot of Madonna in the role of Evita on the front balcony. ⏱ *15 min. See bullet* ①*, p 9.*

⑥ ★★ **El General.** Where else but Buenos Aires could you sit down to lunch at a restaurant surrounded by the Perón political dynasty? This surprisingly good and elegant restaurant is a lunch-time and dinner memorial to the 1945–1955 era of El General Juan Domingo Perón (1895–1974) and the Peronista political movement he and his wife Evita created. It's an unusual but atmospheric place, no matter your political leanings. *Av. Belgrano 561.* ☎ *11/4342-7830. $$.*

⑦ ★★★ **Confitería La Ideal.** This handsomely worn but still-elegant 1912 cafe is part Vienna and all Buenos Aires, the city's most cinematic tango hall (it's not for nothing that many of the most famous films set in Argentina, including *Evita* and *Tango,* used it as a set). While it still operates as a cafe in the morning and early afternoon, at all other hours, it's given over to *la milonga,* tango dances in which everyone can participate, and tango classes. Pop in during the afternoon or evening to check out this hallowed tango shrine, where veterans and newbies find themselves clasped in romantic, rhythmic embraces. ⏱ *1 hr. Suipacha 384, Centro.* ☎ *11/5265-8069. Daily 9am–3am. Admission: Milongas AR$15–AR$25 adults. Subte: Diagonal Norte (C).*

⑧ ★★★ **Cementerio de Recoleta.** Buenos Aires's glorious city of the dead is a place to wander aimlessly, taking in the Gothic, neo-Classical, and Art Nouveau elements of the elaborate mausoleums that house the remains of the city's most

Recoleta cemetery is the final resting place of Eva Perón.

elite citizens and some of the most important figures in Argentine history. But there are several tombs you definitely don't want to miss; see the mini-tour below. ⏱ *1 hr.* *See bullet* ❾, p 18.

Recoleta

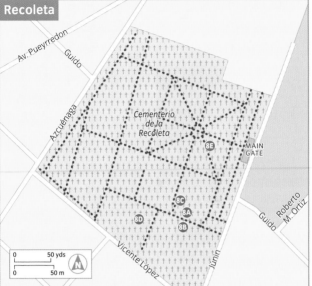

The first constitutional president of Argentina, **8A Bartolomé Mitre,** is buried in a mausoleum guarded by three towering classical figures, a sculpture by Edoardo Rubino (1871–1954). Nearby, Wilfredo Viladrich's (1923–1976) magnificent modern sculpture depicts a young woman, **8B Liliana Crociati,** with her hand resting on her dog's head at the entrance to a small cathedral. A gruesome tale is behind the tomb of Restaurant **Rufina Cambaceres.** According to legend, she suffered a heart attack, went into a coma and was buried, but days later workers heard sounds coming from inside. Her family discovered scratch marks on her face and the inside of her coffin—apparently, she had awoken from her coma to discover herself buried alive. The tomb of Recoleta's biggest draw, **8D Eva Perón,** is down a side alley and identified by her father's family name, Duarte. Her remains were stolen by the military government in 1955 and only returned to her husband in 1971. Since 1976, she has been buried deep beneath the black marble mausoleum—to avoid attempts at robbery. One of Recoleta's most grandiose tombs, a neo-Classical feast of black marble and soaring angels, belongs to **8E José C. Paz,** the owner of the national newspaper *La Prensa.*

The El Ateneo bookstore occupies a 1919 movie theater.

9 ★★ kids **El Ateneo Grand Splendid.** This is surely one of the most remarkable bookstores on the planet, and not because it's some dusty little antique place in a quiet nook of the city. Instead, this shop is grand and splendid in every respect. It occupies a 1919 movie theater, modeled on the Teatre de l'Opera de Paris, and now rows of books occupy three levels that were once box seats. The stage, still adorned with a massive red-velvet curtain, is the site of a cafe-restaurant. You may think you've been cast in a play as you sit sipping your coffee. *Av. Santa Fe 1860, Centro.* ☎ *11/4811-6104. $$.*

10 ★★★ **Museo Evita.** Through stage and film, and the fond memories of her many, many, followers, Eva Perón has become an enduring symbol of Argentina. The force of her cult of personality—as well as her political deeds aimed at disenfranchised workers and women—are on view in this intimate museum about her life, set in a former mansion that was expropriated by the Perón government to serve as a shelter for homeless women and children. Don't miss a chance to enjoy the museum's excellent outdoor cafe around the corner. ⏱ *1hr. See* **5**, *p 23.*

11 ★ kids **Hipódromo de Palermo/Campo Argentino de Polo.** The Argentine fascination with horses isn't limited to the great expanse of the pampas and its mythical gauchos. In the capital, horses mean two things: races at the elegant hipódromo (track) and polo at the Campo Argentino, the "cathedral of polo" since 1893. (Perhaps it's not surprising that the international face of Ralph Lauren Polo is a former polo player from Argentina.) The social upper-class aspect is very much part of the anticipated spectacle at the annual Abierto (Open) matches held in November, but locals take the sport and their teams very seriously. ⏱ *2 hr. Hipódromo: Av. del Libertador 4101, Palermo.* ☎ *11/4778-2839.*

Horse racing at the Hipódromo de Palermo is very popular.

Barbeque food carts along Costanera Sur are popular well into the night.

Races every Mon & Fri from 3pm; check for additional times. Free admission. Campo de Polo: Av. del Libertador (at Av. Dorrego), Palermo. ☎ 11/4576-5600 or 11/4777-8005. www.aapolo.com. Subte: Plaza Italia (D).

12 ★★ **kids Heladería Sarpiecco.** Argentines eat dulce de leche—a rich, thick milk caramel—by the spoonful. You can do that, too (or heap it on toast or try it in crepes), but my favorite way to get a dulce de leche fix is in ice cream (some shops offer a dozen or more flavors of dulce de leche). And my favorite shop is this timeless classic, which has been dispensing artisanal ice cream in the same spot—today considered retro cool with its old-fashioned counters and signs—in Palermo since 1938. *Av. Córdoba 4826, Palermo Soho.* ☎ *11/4773-1829.* $

13 **kids Carritos de la Costanera Sur.** Although much of Buenos Aires has gone upscale, with chic Palermo restaurants and glitzy *parrillas*, more democratic eating traditions live on. One is the colorful barbecue food carts parked along the Costanera Sur, just blocks from Puerto Madero's high-rise apartments and tony yacht club. These amiable joints—which seem to be open 24/7—are favorite haunts of late-night Porteños of all classes, who, after several hours of working or dancing and drinking, drop by to scarf down a *choripán* (chorizo sausage on bread) or *bondiola* (pork) sandwiches. Look for El Parrillón and others with names and smells that you'll probably find awfully difficult to resist. ⏱ *30 min. Av. Achával Rodríguez/Boulevard de los Italianos, Costanera Sur (Puerto Madero). Subte: No access.*

Buenos Aires **for Tango**
Aficionados

Av. E. Madero
Av. Rosales
Av. Leandro N. Alem
L.N. ALEM
Tucumán
Lavalle
San Martín
Florida
Maipú
Viamonte

Azopardo
Parque Colón
Av. Paseo Colón
Balcarce
Defensa
Bolívar
Moreno
Venezuela
Av. Independencia
SAN TELMO
Bolívar
Peru
Chile
Estados Unidos

PLAZA DE MAYO
CATEDRAL
CENTRO MONSERRAT
BOLÍVAR
Av. Roque Sáenz Peña (Diagonal Norte)
Rivadavia
PERÚ
PIEDRAS
Alsina
Moreno
Belgrano
Venezuela
Mexico
Chacabuco
Piedras
Chile
Tacuari
INDEPENDENCIA

CARLOS PELLEGRINI
DIAGONAL NORTE
Florida
Sarmiento
C. Pellegrini
AV. DE MAYO
LIMA
Cerrito
Bernardo de Irigoyen
Av. 9 de Julio
Lima

Plaza Lavalle
Viamonte
C. Pellegrini
Av. 9 de Julio
Libertad
9 DE JULIO
Obelisco
Libertad
Talcahuano
Uruguay
Parana
Montevideo
SAN NICOLÁS
TRIBUNALES
URUGUAY
Rodríguez Peña
Av. Callao
CALLAO
Tucumán
Lavalle

Salta
Santiago del Estero
San José
San José
Pte. Luis Saenz Peña
Carlos Calvo
INDEPENDENCIA
Santiago del Estero
Venezuela
Belgrano
San José
SAENZ PEÑA
CONGRESO
Plaza del Congreso
Solis
Virrey Cevallos
Mexico
Chile
Av. Independencia

FACULTAD DE MEDICINA
Ayacucho
Junin
Pasteur
Azcuenaga
Larrea
San Luis
Av. Pueyrredon
ABASTO
Guardia Vieja
Humacuaca
Agüero
Zelaya
Lavalle
Billinghurst

Riobamba
Riobamba
Av. Corrientes
Tte. General D. Perón
Bartolome Mitre
Sarmiento
P.J.E. Uriburu
Pasteur
Sarmiento
Paso
Castelli
PUEYRREDON
11 DE SEPTIEMBRE STATION
ONCE
Plaza de Miserere
Esparza
LORIA
CARLOS GARDEL

Av. Callao
Ecuador
Anchorena
Ombú
Gallo
Guardia Vieja
ABASTO SHOPPING CENTER

Sarandi
Rincon
Alsina
Moreno
Pichincha
Matheu
Alberti
Adolfo Alsina
Av. Juju
Catamarca
Déan Funes
La Rioja
Plaza 1° de Mayo
Hipolito Yrigoyen
Av. Rivadavia
ALBERTI
PLAZA MISERERE
VENEZUELA
Av. Belgrano
Venezuela

Combate de los Pozos

1/4 mi
0.25 km

Legend
- (i) Information
- (M) Metro Stop
- ■ Point of Interest
- ⊠ Post Office

1 Confiteria La Ideal
2 Tango clothes shopping (Calle Suipacha)
3 Museo Mundial de Tango
4 Café Tortoni
5 El Querandi

6 Abasto barrio
7 Pierino
8 El Niño Bien
9 Esquina Gardel

erhaps no city on Earth is identified with an indigenous art form as Buenos Aires is with tango. For decades, it was considered passé by all but its aging practitioners, but tango has become cool again, especially *la milonga* dancehalls, and young Porteños and international travelers flock to the tango circuit around the city. Besides taking in a *milonga,* you can also visit tango's important landmarks in Buenos Aires. START: **Subte to: Gardel (B), Abasto.**

❶ ★★★ Confiteria La Ideal.
A classic, extravagant 1912 cafe given over to *la milonga* and tango lessons most hours of the day (and featured in the films *Evita* and *Tango*)—including matinee *milongas*—and every day of the week, this is a must-visit for any tango fan. ⏱ *1 hr. See bullet ❼, p 36.*

❷ Tango clothes shopping.
If you're going to hit a *milonga* but forgot to pack your spike heels or sexy skirt, go shopping for authentic tango duds along Calle Suipacha. Top shops include Centro Artesanal del Tango and Zapatos Flabella. ⏱ *45 min. Suipacha 256 & 263, Centro.* ☎ *11/4326-5377 & 11/4322-6036. Subte: Carlos Pellegrini (B).*

❸ Museo Mundial de Tango.
A minor specialist museum for tango fanatics, part of the National Academy of Tango, features instruments, antique tango scores, Gardel's fedora, and assorted tango outfits. ⏱ *30 min. Av. Rivadavia 830, 1st floor, Monserrat.* ☎ *11/4345-6968. www.anacdeltango.org.ar/museo. asp. Admission: AR$3 adults. Mon–Fri 2–8pm. Subte: Av. de Mayo (A).*

❹ ★★★ Café Tortoni.
This venerable cafe, which has welcomed tango giants like Gardel and artists of every persuasion, is a beloved institution. In back is a cool, small theater featuring nightly tango performances. ⏱ *30 min. See bullet ❻, p 10.*

Confiteria La Ideal was featured in the movies Evita *and* Tango.

Tango shoes.

5 ★ **El Querandi.** This historic 1920s Monserrat restaurant offers a quite good and intimate dinner-theater program that tells the story of tango's birth and evolution. If you're more in the mood for a glass of wine, the restaurant recently opened a wine bar next door. *Perú 302.* ☎ *11/5199-1770. $$*

6 ★ **Abasto barrio.** This neighborhood is intimately identified with tango. Carlos Gardel, the greatest star tango produced, frequented it and lived the last years of his life here. Today, the barrio is pulling out all the stops to make its tango connection colorfully appealing, much as La Boca has with Caminito. *Neighborhood tours Sat at 4:30pm; meeting point Corrientes 3190. Free admission Reservations* ☎ *11/6311-4461.*

7 ★ **Pierino.** Astor Piazzolla (1921–1992), a bandoneón player and composer who revolutionized tango music with "Tango Nuevo" (which he described as music to

listen to and contemplate, rather than dance to), was a regular at this family-run and photo-filled Italian restaurant, which dates to 1909. *Lavalle 3499.* ☎ *11/4864-5715. $$.*

8 ★★★ **Milonga circuit.** Whether you're a practiced tango dancer ready to strap on your dancing shoes, or just want to watch others—both natives and groups of foreigners who've moved to Buenos Aires to join the informal circuit—you'll find classic old-school *milongas* every night of the week (they start around 11pm and go as late as 6am). The principal dance halls, each with their own night of prominence and dedicated followers, are Niño Bien (Constitución/San Telmo; Thurs), which is perhaps the most famous of its kind. Others sought out by aficionados are:, Salón Canning and La Viruta (Palermo Viejo; Fri and Sun), Club Gricel (San Cristobal; Fri), Sunderland (Villa Urquiza; Sat), and the outdoor pavilion at La Glorieta in Belgrano (Sun). *See p 117 for listings.*

Abasto

ABASTO

San Luis
Tucumán
Aguero
Viamonte
Gallo
Zelaya
Tucumán
Lavalle
Anchorena
6D
Guardia Vieja
6F
6E
Humacuaca
ABASTO
SHOPPING
CENTER
6C
CARLOS
GARDEL
6B
B
Jean Jaures
Ecuador
Boulogne Sur Mer
Av. Pueyrredon
6A
PUEYRREDON
B

0   1/8 mi
0   0.125 km

The 6A **Subte Carlos Gardel** (subway stop) in front of Mercado del Abasto is named for the tango legend, and murals in the station memorialize the singer. 6B **Esquina Fileteada** is emblazoned with dozens of *fileteado* illustrations, a native art form that is now a visual expression of tango culture. One of the city's top tango music-and-dance shows, 6C **Esquina Carlos Gardel,** inhabits the 1893 cantina Chanta Cuatro, where Gardel was a regular. Abasto's answer to La Boca's Caminito is 6D **Pasaje Zelaya,** a colorful street of squat pastel houses, adorned with famous tango lyrics and Gardel's fedora-topped visage. 6E ★★ **Paseo del Fileteado** is a solid block of *fileteado* painting, with houses on either side of the street done up in colorful swirls. 6F ★ kids **Museo-Casa Carlos Gardel** occupies the small "chorizo-style" house (long and narrow, like a sausage) where Gardel lived with his mother in the 1930s until moving to Paris shortly before his death. Today, it's a museum, with instruments, records, songbooks, and artwork. *Jean Jaurés 735.* ☎ *11/4964-2015. Admission: AR$1 adults. Mon & Wed–Fri 11am–7pm; Sat–Sun 10am–7pm.*

❾ ★ **Tangueria.** The Broadway version of tango, these well-produced nightly music-and-dance shows feature sleek, skin-baring dancers and orchestras (though purists deride them as "tango for export"). They vary from intimate to big dinner musical productions. One of the best is Esquina Gardel (Abasto), although El Viejo Almacén (San Telmo), and Piazzola Tango (Centro) also put on very fine shows. See p 129 for listings.

Buenos Aires Architecture &

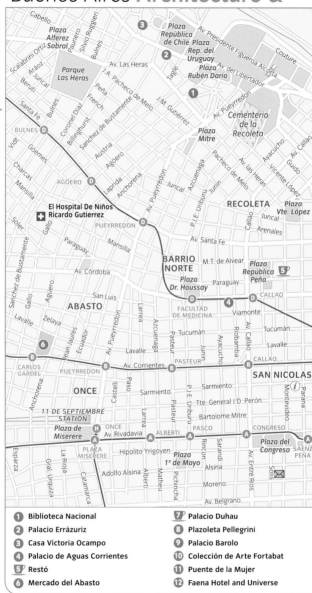

1. Biblioteca Nacional
2. Palacio Errázuriz
3. Casa Victoria Ocampo
4. Palacio de Aguas Corrientes
5. Restó
6. Mercado del Abasto
7. Palacio Duhau
8. Plazoleta Pellegrini
9. Palacio Barolo
10. Colección de Arte Fortabat
11. Puente de la Mujer
12. Faena Hotel and Universe

Design

Av. Presidente Ramón S. Castillo

Av. Antártida Argentina

Av. Comodoro Py

🛑 Hospital
ⓘ Information
Ⓜ Metro Stop
⬛ Point of Interest
✉ Post Office

Padre Mujica

RETIRO STATION
ⓘ
C RETIRO

Av. Ramos Mejía

San Martín

Av. Antártida Argentina

Av. del Libertador

Posadas
Montevideo
Av. Alvear
Av. Quintana

7

8

Autopista Arturo Illia

Arroyo

Juncal

Arenales

Av. Santa Fe

ⓘ **C** SAN MARTÍN
M.T. de Alvear

RETIRO

Av. Maipú

Torre de los Ingleses ⬛
Plaza San Martín

Av. E. Madero

Av. Leandro N. Alem

Darsena Norte

Av. de los Italianos
Juana Manso

Av. Int. Hernán M. Giralt

Plaza Libertad

Av. 9 de Julio

C. Pellegrini

Paraguay

ⓘ
Av. Córdoba

Av. Córdoba

Viamonte

San Martín

Florida

Tucumán

Av. E. Madero

10
Dique No. 4

Plaza Lavalle

D TRIBUNALES

Suipacha
Maipú

LAVALLE **C**

Lavalle
L.N. ALEM

Av. Leandro N. Alem

Av. Rosales

D
B Obelisco
B URUGUAY

✉
9 DE JULIO
D
C

CARLOS PELLEGRINI

Av. Corrientes

FLORIDA

Reconquista

B

Av. Alicia Moreau de Justo

Av. Macacha Güemes

Uruguay
Talcahuano
Libertad
Cerrito

DIAGONAL NORTE
Sarmiento

San Martín

Av. Roque Sáenz Peña (Diagonal Norte)

11
Dique No. 3

Parque Mujeres Argentinas

9
Av. de Mayo
Santiago del Estero
San José

Lima
Talcahuano

C. Pellegrini

Av. 9 de Julio

Bernardo de Irigoyen

Rivadavia
ⓘ **A**
PERÚ

A PLAZA DE MAYO

CENTRO-MONSERRAT
CATEDRAL

A
AV. DE MAYO
PIEDRAS **E** BOLÍVAR

Alsina

Parque Colón

C
MORENO **E**

Av. Julio A. Rocha (Diagonal Sur)

Moreno

Balcarce

Av. Paseo Colón

Azopardo

Bvd. A. Villaflor

PUERTO MADERO

Av. Belgrano

BELGRANO

Av. Belgrano

Defensa

Venezuela

Av. Ing. Huergo

Dique No. 2

Aimé Paine

Venezuela

Piedras
Chacabuco

Mexico ✉

Bolívar
Perú

SAN TELMO

12

Salta
Santiago del Estero
San José

INDEPENDENCIA

Lima
Av. 9 de Julio

Tacuari

Chile

E
C
INDEPENDENCIA

Av. Independencia

Estados Unidos

Balcarce

Carlos Calvo

In its heyday in the early 20th century, Buenos Aires was wealthy and grand, the Paris of South America—with the Belle Epoque architecture and wide boulevards to back up that claim. And while the city hasn't been known for its modern architecture, that's beginning to change. Today, it's an attractive mix of old and new, European and Latin American. START: **Taxi to Av. del Libertador (at Agüero), Palermo.**

1 Biblioteca Nacional. Most Porteños disparage the National Library, moved to Palermo from its historic home in Monserrat, as an embarrassing eyesore. Though it opened only in 1992, the top-heavy design by the Italian architect Clorindo Testa seems emphatically late 1960s or 1970s in its inspiration. And with good reason: Construction actually began in 1971, but bureaucratic snafus prevented it from getting built, ensuring that it was already vintage upon inauguration. ⏲ *15 min. Agüero 2502, Palermo.* ☎ *11/4806-4721. www.bibnal.edu. ar. Subte: No access.*

The Museo Nacional de Arte Decorativo is located inside an early 20th-century French-style mansion.

2 ★★★ Palacio Errázuriz. The only early-20th-century French-styled mansion in Buenos Aires open to the public, this grand 1918 structure by René Sergent (1865–1927), the French architect who also built the nearby U.S. embassy, is now home to the **Museo Nacional de Arte Decorativo.** It features an English Tudor Grand Hall with a massive fireplace (which was to have been designed by Auguste Rodin [1840–1917], who couldn't agree on a price); baroque Louis XV–style dining room; Regency-style ballroom; and the son's Art Deco bedroom, designed (paintings and all) by the Catalan painter Josep María Sert (1876–1945). All materials were shipped from Europe. ⏲ *1 hr. See bullet 1, p 21.*

3 ★ Casa Victoria Ocampo. Standing out from Palermo Chico's grand homes and embassies is this stark 1929 home, considered the first expression of modernism in Buenos Aires. It was once home to Victoria Ocampo (1890–1979), an early admirer of Le Corbusier (1887–1965) and a prominent intellectual who founded the literary journal *Sur* here. After she attended Le Corbusier's series of lectures in the city, Ocampo commissioned a less-than-enthusiastic Alejandro Bustillo (1889–1982) to carry out her ideals. The home now hosts the Fondo Nacional de las Artes, a foundation featuring contemporary art exhibits and lectures. ⏲ *30 min. Rufino de Elizalde 2831, Palermo Chico.* ☎ *11/4808-0553. www.fnartes.gov.ar. Free admission.*

Tues–Fri 3–7pm; Sat–Sun 1–7pm. Subte: No access.

④ ★★ Palacio de Aguas Corrientes. Another landmark building whose opulent exterior camouflaged prosaic goings-on inside, this imposing and richly detailed, block-long 1894 building originally stored massive tanks with the city's water supply and mechanisms for water purification. Yet not for nothing is it referred to as a "palace." Today, behind the eclectic exterior of 300,000 ceramic and red brick pieces—shipped from England and Belgium, and pieced together like a puzzle—is a quirky museum detailing the history of Buenos Aires from the point of view of its water supply, something few of us probably give much thought to. If nothing else, it contains perhaps the most impressive collection of toilets you've ever seen. ⏱ *45 min. Riobamba 750 (at Av. Córdoba), Barrio Norte.* ☎ *11/6319-1104. www.aysa.com.ar. Free admission. Tours daily 11am. Subte: Callao (D).*

The Palacio de Aguas Corrientes houses a quirky museum inside its opulent exterior.

⑤ ★★★ Restó. This outstanding small restaurant, with a young woman chef at the helm and open for lunch Monday to Friday and dinner on Thursday and Friday, is the perfect pit stop for an architectural tour: It's tucked within Buenos Aires's Central Society of Architects, so plenty of your fellow diners will have similar interests. *Montevideo 938, Barrio Norte.* ☎ *11/4816-6711. $$$*

⑥ ★ kids Mercado del Abasto. This landmark structure, a 46,452-square-meter (500,000-sq.-ft.) Art Deco masterpiece from 1934, was originally the city's central fruit and vegetable market. Transformed into a modern shopping center in 1999, it retains its distinctive roofline of five arcs, which gives it the appearance of a railway

station. ⏱ *30 min. Av. Corrientes 3247, Abasto.* ☎ *11/4959-3400. Subte: Carlos Gardel (B).*

⑦ ★★ Palacio Duhau. This magnificent 1934 palace, now incorporated into the Park Hyatt Hotel, is a refined place for afternoon tea in the elegant Piano Nobile salons, overlooking the gardens, with fireplace and original painted boiserie (carved-wood paneling). Some men, though, might prefer the hyper-masculine Oak Bar for a drink and a Cuban cigar. *Av. Alvear 1661.* ☎ *11/5171-1351. $$$.*

⑧ ★★ Plazoleta Pellegrini. Av. Alvear, Buenos Aires's most elegant avenue, has plenty of show-stopping buildings, like the Alvear Palace hotel. But the far end, just before reaching Av. 9 de Julio, is my

This modern shopping center used to be the city's central fruit and vegetable market.

favorite section. The lovely and quiet small square, Plazoleta Pellegrini, looks as if it is straight out of Paris (no doubt the reason the French embassy is located here, in a beautiful Belle Epoque mansion). Also on the square is the Brazilian embassy, and just around the corner, on Posadas, is La Mansión, an opulent mansion that now belongs to the Four Seasons Hotel. 🕐 *30 min. Av. Alvear (at Cerrito), La Recoleta. Subte: San Martín (C).*

⑨ ★★★ **Palacio Barolo.** A 22-story "palace" on one of Buenos Aires's most distinguished avenues, this neo-Gothic 1923 skyscraper (the tallest building in the city until 1935 and the first made from reinforced concrete) by the Italian architect Mario Palanti (1885–1979) is original outside and sumptuous within. Take a tour or ride an old-school elevator to the Tango Moda shop on the 16th floor for incredible panoramic views of the palace's cupola and all of Buenos Aires (including, from up here, the seemingly tiny Obelisco on Av. 9 de Julio). Most curiously, Palanti designed the building as an homage to Dante's *The Divine Comedy* (see p 49). 🕐 *1 hr. See bullet* ⑧, *p 12.*

⑩ ★★★ **kids Colección de Arte Fortabat.** A sparkling new art museum in Puerto Madero, opened in October 2008, is encased in Rafael Viñoly's stunning, technologically advanced, 557-square-meter (6,000-sq.-ft.) design. The concrete, glass, and steel cylinder lies on its side and looks something like a cement mixer—which might not be unexpected, since the private art collection on view belongs to a woman who made her fortune in cement. Upstairs, computer-controlled aluminum shades open and close in

The 16th floor of Edificio Barolo gives incredible panoramic views of the city.

response to the position of the sun, admitting an abundance of natural light but protecting the works while providing splendid panoramic views of the port area and yacht club. 🕐 *1 hr. See bullet ⑦, p 18.*

⑪ ★ **Puente de la Mujer.** The celebrated Spanish architect Santiago Calatrava, world-renowned for his transportation hubs and bridges on several continents, contributed this minimalist, 102-meter-long (335-ft.-long) suspension walkway, called "Bridge of the Woman," to Puerto Madero in 2001. The central portion of the asymmetrical bridge can rotate 90 degrees to allow water traffic to pass. Some have interpreted the design as an abstract homage to a couple dancing tango. 🕐 *20 min. Dique (Dock) 3 (between Azucena Villaflor & Machacha Güemes), Puerto Madero. Subte: L.N. Alem (B).*

⑫ ★★ **Faena Hotel and Universe.** The trendy fashionistas' hotel of choice is this chic hotel, owned by the Argentine fashion designer Alan Faena, housed in a 1902 brick granary and enlivened by Philippe Starck's daring interior designs of dramatically lit hallways and whimsical rooms. The flamboyant restaurant is a monochromatic

The Colección de Arte Fortabat has shades that open and close in response to the position of the sun.

study in white, with unicorn heads on the walls, while the pool bar—at the entrance to the hotel—is where the famously beautiful hang out to see and be seen. The staff can get a little touchy about letting plebes in, so head to the bar. Across the street, a new hotel and apartment project is going up, the first in Latin America by Sir Norman Foster, and a partnership with Faena. 🕐 *45 min. Martha Salotti 445, Puerto Madero.* ☎ *11/4010-9000. www.faenahotel anduniverse.com. Subte: No access.*

A Divinely Inspired Skyscraper

If you gaze up at the Palacio Barolo and think, "divine," well, you're right on the money. The Italian architect, Mario Palanti, belonged to the fraternal order La Fede Santa (Sacred Faith), of which the legendary poet Dante Alighieri, centuries earlier, was also a member. Palanti was quite evidently a fan of Dante; his building reaches skyward to embody Dante's epic poem The Divine Comedy. The 22-storey skyscraper features three distinct sections, as does the poem, representing hell, purgatory, and paradise. The building height, 100 meters (328 ft.), is equal to the 100 cantos of the poem. Each floor contains either 11 or 22 offices, just as Dante's cantos had either 11 or 22 stanzas.

Buenos Aires **for Kids**

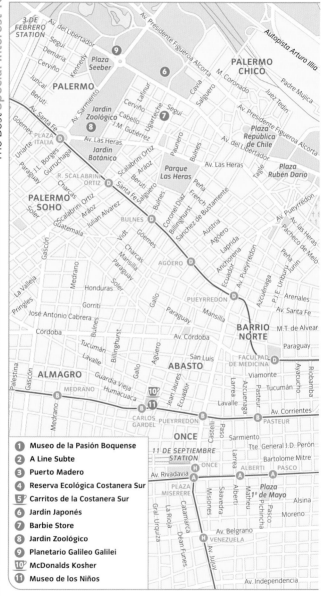

1. Museo de la Pasión Boquense
2. A Line Subte
3. Puerto Madero
4. Reserva Ecológica Costanera Sur
5. Carritos de la Costanera Sur
6. Jardín Japonés
7. Barbie Store
8. Jardín Zoológico
9. Planetario Galileo Galilei
10. McDonalds Kosher
11. Museo de los Niños

Buenos Aires is a well laid-out and kid-friendly city, especially for an extremely large capital (more than 13 million inhabitants). From *fútbol* to wide-open parks and a well-designed museum for kids, it shouldn't be hard for families to keep the kids entertained. And who knows? Maybe they'll take to tango. START: **Taxi to Brandsen 805, La Boca.**

① ★ **Museo de la Pasión Boquense.** Kids that play and love soccer can visit one of the sport's temples, the colossal 1940 stadium known as La Bombonera, home to Maradona's former team, Boca Juniors. The museum in the basement of the stadium is an entertaining stroll through Boca Juniors history and paraphernalia, followed by a visit to the cavernous stadium. If you attend a match with kids, though, be careful; Boca fans can get very rowdy. ⏱ *1 hr. See bullet* **①**, *p 34.*

② ★★★ **A Line Subte.** Kids will love this rickety ride through history, on the original wooden cars (from 1913) of South America's oldest subway. Grab a hand ring and hold on; it's the next best thing to a rollercoaster. Families will appreciate the retro stylings at the Perú station, done up in authentic period charm. (Note that some newer cars have been introduced on the line, so wait for one of the older cars.) ⏱ *20 min. See bullet* **⑩**, *p 12.*

③ ★★ **Puerto Madero.** The epicenter of new office and residential towers might not seem like much of a draw for children, but the old warehouse and port district has several diverting features. Two old docked wooden ships, the **Fragata *Presidente Sarmiento*** and **Corbeta *Uruguay*,** 19th-century vessels that sailed as far away as Antarctica, now function as naval museums and can be boarded. Tall, brightly colored cranes punctuate the entire zone; though they make it look like everything's under construction, these were erected as a playful acknowledgment of the zone's building frenzy of recent years. And the stark-white pedestrian bridge, **Puente de la Mujer,** is fun to cross—check out the yachts and skyscrapers in the distance. ⏱ *1 hr. Diques 3/4. Puerto Madero.* ☎ *11/4314-1090 or 11/4334-9386. www.ara.mil.ar. Subte: No access.*

The museum inside La Bombonera is great for soccer lovers.

Kids can feed the fish in the Jardín Japonés.

④ ★ Reserva Ecológica Costanera Sur. This wetlands preserve at the outer edge of upscale, still-being-built Puerto Madero is a place to leave the city behind, with walking and bicycling paths that lead down to the wide and muddy Río de la Plata (though it's a very long walk for small children). There's good bird-watching (with more than 250 resident species), but don't dare let the kids go into the polluted river. ⏱ *1 hr. Av. Achával Rodríguez, Puerto Madero.* ☎ *11/4893-1588. Subte: No access.*

⑤ Carritos de la Costanera Sur. These colorful, open-air barbecue food carts parked along the Costanera Sur are the perfect stop for an Argentine version of the hot dog: a *choripán* (chorizo sausage on bread). *Av. Achával Rodríguez/Boulevard de los Italianos, Costanera Sur, Puerto Madero. $.*

⑥ ★ Jardín Japonés. These Zen-like, landscaped Japanese gardens are a great place for kids to romp around in a closed environment. They can play on red bowed bridges, leap onto rock islands, feed wide-mouthed carp, and learn about origami in the cultural center. ⏱ *1 hr. Av. Figueroa Alcorta (at Av. Casares), Palermo.* ☎ *11/4804-9141. www.jardinjapones.com. Admission: AR $5 adults; AR$1 children ages 6–10. Daily 10am–6pm. Subte: Plaza Italia (D).*

⑦ ★ Barbie Store. Buenos Aires is the proud destination of the world's first store dedicated to all things Barbie, and all pink, all the time. It has a Barbie beauty salon, tea house, and Casa Barbie for birthday parties. Little girls (or boys, as

19th-century ships now in Puerto Madero sailed as far away as Antarctica.

Buenos Aires is home to the world's first Barbie store.

well) will go wild; it's like they become Barbie (scary as that might be for parents). ⏱ *30 min. Scalabrini Ortiz 3170, Palermo.* ☎ *0810/4444-BARBIE. www.barbie-stores.com. Mon–Sat 10am–8:30pm; Sun 1–8pm. Subte: Plaza Italia (D).*

8 ★★ **Jardín Zoológico.** Unless you're philosophically opposed to all zoos, this one, which opened in 1888, is a good one, with buildings supposed to represent the animals' native countries (like the elephants' Indian temple). There are polar bears, big cats, and indigenous South American species, including vicuñas and condors, as well as zoo-keeper talks, guided visits in English, and occasional night visits. ⏱ *2 hrs. Av. Sarmiento (at Av. Las Heras), Palermo.* ☎ *11/4011-9999. www.zoobuenosaires.com.ar. Admission: AR$9–AR$16 adults; free for children 11 and under. Mar–Dec Tues–Sun 10am–6pm (last entrance 5pm); Jan–Feb daily. Subte: Plaza Italia (D).*

9 ★★ **Planetario Galileo Galilei.** The geodesic dome in the midst of Palermo's garden district isn't a docked spaceship, it's the planetarium, built in the early 1960s and a charming throwback. It features entertaining shows (in Spanish) about the Southern Hemisphere constellations and comets, as well as telescope observations on Sundays. ⏱ *1 hr. Av. Sarmiento (at Av.*

The Jardín Zoológico has many indigenous South American species.

Alcorta), Palermo. ☎ *11/4771-9393.*
www.planetario.gov.ar. Admission:
AR$4 adults; free seniors & children
2 and under. Shows Tues–Fri 5pm &
6pm; Sat–Sun 2, 3, & 4:30pm. Tele-
scope: Sun 7:30–9:30pm. Subte:
Plaza Italia (D).

🔟 **McDonalds Kosher.** Within
the Mercado de Abasto shopping
center is a rarity: an all-kosher
Mickey D's—the first such fast-food
restaurant outside Israel and a rec-
ognition of the barrio's large Jewish
population. *Av. Corrientes 3247 (2nd*
floor), Abasto. ☎ *11/4959-3709. $.*

⓫ ★★ **Museo de los Niños.**
Tucked away inside the Abasto
Shopping Center, this children's
museum puts the world of adults in
kids' hands. They get to play at
grownup careers, from miniature
dentist's and doctor's offices to
working TV and radio stations. Buenos Aires is represented, too, with
miniature versions of the Casa
Rosada and Congreso. Scatalogi-
cally-minded kids will love the giant

Kids get to play at being grown-ups
at the children's museum.

toilet, where they get to plunge into
the process of sewage. Eww. ⏱ *2*
hrs. Av. Corrientes 3247 (2nd floor),
Abasto. ☎ *11/4861-2325. Admis-*
sion AR$15–AR$20 adults; free for
seniors & children 2 and under; spe-
cial pricing for families. Tues–Sun
1–8pm. Subte: Gardel (B).

Out-of-Town Excursions for Families

Though there's plenty in Buenos Aires to entertain children of all
ages, a couple of excursions are great for families with additional
time in the city. The delightful Tren de la Costa that goes north to
Tigre and the River Delta (see p 146) is a fun trip for kids, as are the
boat trips to the islands in the Delta, but there's also a popular
amusement park, Parque de la Costa, right across from the train
depot. About 50 km (31 miles), or about 30 minutes, outside Buenos
Aires is Bioparque Temaikén (Ruta Provincial 25, km. 1, Escobar;
☎ 03488-436900; www.temaiken.com; admission: AR $35 adults,
AR$23 seniors and children ages 3–10; Tues half-price), an excellent
wildlife park with 200 species, including tigers, pumas, reptiles, and
penguins, living in open spaces. Kids will also enjoy a visit to an
estancia (country estate) and the opportunity to go horseback riding on the Argentine pampas (see p 154).

Buenos Aires for Art Lovers

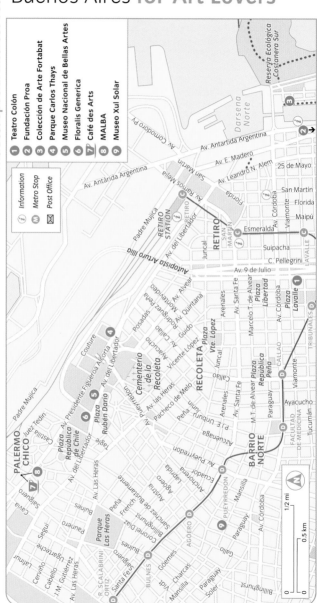

1 Teatro Colón
2 Fundación Proa
3 Colección de Arte Fortabat
4 Parque Carlos Thays
5 Museo Nacional de Bellas Artes
6 Floralis Generica
7 Café des Arts
8 MALBA
9 Museo Xul Solar

ⓘ Information
Ⓜ Metro Stop
☒ Post Office

An art tour of Buenos Aires isn't the expected traipsing through exhausting art museums with monumental international collections. Buenos Aires offers a unique chance to discover Argentine and Latin American artists in smaller and more personal museums—and one spectacular opera house. START: **Subte to: Tribunales (D).**

1 ★★★ **Teatro Colón.** One of the world's great opera houses, inaugurated in 1908, recently celebrated its centennial while still under wraps during a multi-year restoration. The world's greatest artists and singers, including Callas, Strauss, Nureyev, and Caruso, have performed at this gorgeous hall with renowned acoustics, luxurious salons, and a painted dome. See a performance, if at all possible, or tour the beautifully restored 3,000-seat building, including backstage and costume areas. ⏱ *1 hr. Libertad 621, Centro.* ☎ *11/4378-7344 or, for tour information, 11/4378-7130. Admission: AR$15 adults. Tours weekdays 11am–3pm; Sat 9am–noon. Hours may change after reopening. www.teatrocolon.org.ar. Subte: Tribunales (D).*

2 ★★ **Fundación Proa.** This progressive-minded art foundation hosts excellent exhibits of contemporary international artists (such as Marcel Duchamp, Jenny Holzer, Sol LeWitt, and Sebastião Salgado) in an ingeniously converted Italianate mansion with a modern glass addition and nod to the area's edgy past. ⏱ *1 hr. See bullet* **1**, *p 15.*

The Colección de Arte Fortabat has some of the biggest names in international and Argentine artists of the last 100 years.

3 ★★ **Colección de Arte Fortabat.** This stunning new museum houses the private art collection of one of Argentina's richest women, Amalia Lacroze de Fortabat. Her extensive holdings include some of the biggest names among international and Argentine artists of the last 100 years, including Andy Warhol (1928–1987), who painted Fortabat; Rodin; Marc Chagall (1887–1985); Salvador Dalí (1904–1989); J.M.W. Turner (1775–1851); and Berni, as well as 4,000-year-old Egyptian pieces. ⏱ *1 hr. See bullet* **7**, *p 18.*

4 **Parque Carlos Thays.** In homage to the early-20th-century French landscape designer instrumental to so many green zones of Buenos Aires, this park of tall trees is distinguished by a large bust by the Colombian artist Fernando Botero (1932–). ⏱ *1 hr. Av. Libertador (at Av. Callao), Palermo. Subte: No access.*

5 ★★ **Museo Nacional de Bellas Artes.** Argentina's most important art museum may not be the Met, but it has a good roster of European art (Rembrandt, Monet, El Greco, van Gogh, and Picasso) and the largest collection of 19th- and 20th-century Argentine art—all in a building that, prior to 1933, was the pump station for the city's water supply. ⏱ *1 hr. Av. del Libertador 1473, Palermo.* ☎ *11/4803-0802. www.mnba.org.ar. Free admission. Tues–Fri 12:30–7:30pm; Sat–Sun 9:30am–9:30pm. Subte: No access.*

6 ★ Floralis Generica. Candidate for new symbol of the city, Eduardo Catalano's huge, 20-meter-high (66-ft.) steel-and-aluminum 2002 sculpture of a "generic flower" opens at the beginning of each day and closes at sunset (though 4 days a year, it remains open: May 25, Sept 21, and Dec 24 and 25). ⏱ *15 min. Plaza de las Naciones Unidas, Av. Figueroa Alcorta (at Austria). Free admission. Daily 8am–8pm. Subte: No access.*

7 ★★ Café des Arts. Within MALBA (see below) is this terrific modern French bistro, a great (and unexpectedly sophisticated) lunch spot with a relaxing outdoor terrace. *Av. Figueroa Alcorta 3415.* ☎ *11/4808-0754. $$$.*

8 ★★ MALBA. Local businessman Eduardo Costantini's extensive private collection carries the impressive name Museo de Arte Latinoamericano de Buenos Aires. Both the modern building and the collection live up to the name, with major

modern Latin American artists represented, including Diego Rivera (1886–1957), Frida Kahlo (1907–1954), Roberto Matta (1911–2002), Tarsila do Amaral (1886–1973), Fernando Botero (1932–), and Wilfredo Lam (1902–1982), as well the Argentines Antonio Berni (1905–1981) and Xul Solar (1887–1963). ⏱ *1 hr. See bullet 3, p 22.*

9 ★★ Museo Xul Solar. The eccentric Argentine painter and sculptor, who adopted the name Xul Solar, lived and worked in this 100-year-old home, transformed into a handsome space and highly personal museum of his work. Solar, a part-time mathematician and astrologist with wide-ranging intellectual interests—among other things, he invented two nonsense languages—was a close friend of Jorge Luis Borges and himself a leading light of the avant-garde in Argentina. The collection is not only of his colorful work, which owes a debt to Paul Klee (1879–1940) and Wassily Kandinsky (1866–1944), but a variety of peculiar objects and instruments. ⏱ *1 hr. Laprida 1212, Palermo.* ☎ *11/4824-3302. www.xulsolar.org.ar. Admission: AR $6 adults; AR$2 seniors & students. Tues–Fri noon–7:30pm; Sat noon–7pm. Guided tours: Tues & Thur 4pm; Sat 3:30pm. Subte: No access.* ●

This huge flower sculpture opens at sunrise and closes at sunset.

60

The Best Neighborhood Walks

Avenida de Mayo

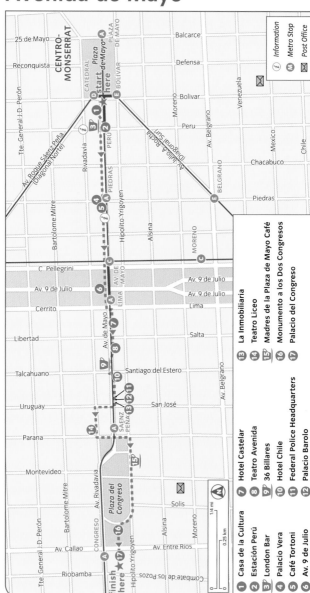

Legend:
- ⓘ Information
- Ⓜ Metro Stop
- ☒ Post Office

CENTRO-
MONSERRAT

Start Plaza de Mayo here

1 Casa de la Cultura
2 Estación Perú
3 London Bar
4 Palacio Vera
5 Café Tortoni
6 Av. 9 de Julio
7 Hotel Castelar
8 Teatro Avenida
9 36 Billares
10 Hotel Chile
11 Federal Police Headquarters
12 Palacio Barolo
13 La Inmobiliaria
14 Teatro Liceo
15 Madres de la Plaza de Mayo Café
16 Monumento a los Dos Congresos
17 Palacio del Congreso

finish here ★

Plaza del Congreso

1/4 mi
0.25 km

Previous Page: A painted horse outside the Alvear Palace Hotel.

The historic center's elegant thoroughfare, Av. de Mayo, connects Argentina's two most important houses of government, Casa Rosada and Palacio del Congreso. Designed in the late 19th century to mimic Paris's grand boulevards, the avenue is lined with splendid examples of Beaux Arts, Art Nouveau, and European-influenced architecture, as well as some of the city's most atmospheric cafes and old hotels and theaters. START: **Subte to Catedral (D) or Perú (A).**

1 ★★ **Casa de la Cultura.** A French Garnier–style building from 1889, this is the former headquarters of the prestigious national newspaper *La Prensa.* Take a look at the ornate lanterns, lion-head door knockers, and bronze statue gracing the top and advocating for freedom of the press. Today, the building houses the Argentine Ministry of Culture; occasional performances are held in the Versailles-like salon. *See bullet* **5**, *p 10.*

2 ★★ **Estación Perú.** Beneath the whole of Av. de Mayo runs the historic **A line** of the *subte* (subway), the first built in South America. The 1913 Peru station has been restored to period authenticity with early-20th-century advertising posters, red-and-cream-colored kiosks, and original turnstiles.

3 **London Bar.** Julio Cortázar (1914–1984), Argentina's most famous modern novelist, wrote parts of *Los Premios* (The Winners) at this classic 1954 cafe and patisserie, which itself makes an appearance in the 1960 book. *Av. de Mayo 559.* ☎ *11/4342-9057. $.*

4 ★ **Palacio Vera.** At no. 767 is one of the boulevard's loveliest examples of Art Nouveau architecture, a 1910 palace that was originally the home of the prominent Díaz Vélez family. Check out the splendid details on the balconies. *Av. de Mayo 767.*

5 ★★★ **Café Tortoni.** Buenos Aires's oldest cafe, opened by a French immigrant, is rightly famous and a must-stop for every visitor to the city—previous visitors include Carlos Gardel (1890–1935), Jorge Luis Borges (1899–1986), and Federico García Lorca (1898–1936). The cafe's mid-19th-century grandeur predates Av. de Mayo by more than 3 decades. *See bullet* **6**, *p 10.*

6 ★ **Av. 9 de Julio.** At 140 meters (459 ft.) wide, this is routinely celebrated as the widest street in the world and is named for the date of Argentina's independence from Spain—its 16 lanes can also be a challenge to cross. One of the defining symbols of the city, the towering **Obelisco,** rises from the middle of the avenue—at the spot where the Argentine flag was raised for the first time—4 blocks north of the Av. de Mayo intersection.

Performances are occassionally held in the French-style Casa de la Cultura.

The Obelisco stands in the middle of Avenida 9 de Julio.

7 Hotel Castelar. This classic 1929 hotel, at no. 1152, is where the great Spanish writer Federico García Lorca lived (in room 704) in 1933 and 1934. The hotel, designed by Mario Palanti (1885–1979), the architect of the acclaimed Palacio Barolo down the street, retains its old-school flavor. *Av. de Mayo 1152.*

8 Teatro Avenida. At no. 1222, this grand 1908 theater—where Lorca staged his work *Blood Wedding*—was one of the most important in the city until a fire closed it for 15 years. It was finally restored and reopened in 1994, though much of its former glory had gone up in smoke. *Av. de Mayo 1222.*

9 ★★ Los 36 Billares. Opened the same year as Av. de Mayo (1894), this venerable cafe has another world operating downstairs—one you might not know about if you just stopped for a coffee and didn't pay attention to the name—where older gentlemen come to shoot pool day and night. *Av. de Mayo 1265. 11/4381-5696. $$.*

10 Hotel Chile. One of the most exceptional Art Nouveau buildings in Buenos Aires is this formerly grand hotel, at no. 1297, with wrought-iron balconies and glazed ornamental tiling of Middle Eastern influence. Designed by the French architect Jules Dubois (1888–1958) in 1907, it suffered a devastating fire in the cupola. Today, it's a budget hotel, although one with elegant bones. *Av. de Mayo 1297.*

11 Federal Police Headquarters. I'm not sending you to the slammer; this police building at no. 1333 now occupies what was the 1926 headquarters of the left-wing *Crítica* newspaper, to which Jorge Luis Borges was a contributor. The building is a rare example of Art Deco styling, with neo-Egyptian sculptures and geometric shapes. *Av. de Mayo 1333.*

12 ★★★ kids Palacio Barolo. This marvelous 22-story building, the tallest in South America when opened in 1923, was designed by the eccentric Italian architect Mario Palanti to pay homage to Dante's *The Divine Comedy.* Peek inside at the luxurious lobby and ride one of the antique elevators to the top. *See bullet 8, p 12 & box, p 4.*

Los historic 36 Billares boasts a café upstairs and a pool hall in the basement.

13 La Inmobiliaria. This monumental 1910 building, designed as offices for a real estate insurance company, is distinguished by its twin red cupolas. Note the Art Nouveau tile sign at the top of the façade, proof of its former life. *Av. de Mayo 1400.*

14 Teatro Liceo. Just off Av. de Mayo, at Rivadavia 1495, this grand 1866 theater—the oldest in Buenos Aires—is where a young actress named Eva Duarte performed, only a few years before she would become much better known as Evita Perón (1919–1952). *Rivadavia 1495.*

15 ★ Madres de la Plaza de Mayo Café. The Mothers of the Plaza de Mayo have their headquarters here and operate a bookstore and cafe, which fund their activities on policy issues. The Mothers continue to insist that the government take responsibility for the disappearance and murder of as many as 30,000 people at the hands of the military juntas of the 1970s and 1980s. *Yrigoyen 1584.* ☎ 11/4382-3261. *See bullet* **4**, *p 35.*

16 ★ Monumento a los Dos Congresos. A sumptuous marble-and-bronze monument and fountains, made in Belgium in 1908, commemorate the 1810 and 1816

The design of Palacio Barolo pays homage to Dante's Divine Comedy.

congresses held after independence was declared from Spain, instrumental in establishing the framework for the new nation of Argentina. *Av. Entre Ríos at Rivadavia.*

17 ★★ Palacio del Congreso. The imposing 1906 neo-Classical Congress building houses the Senate and House of Representatives. It is a pastiche of influences, from the U.S. Capitol to Paris's Garnier Opera House and Berlin's Brandenburg Gate. *See bullet* **9**, *p 12.*

From Destruction to Ground Zero

When Av. de Mayo was constructed in 1894, it ended where the Plaza Congreso now stands. But Carlos Thays's (1839–1934) 1910 design for this immense square—to commemorate the centennial of the May Revolution of 1810—required the destruction of several opulent office and apartment buildings that had been built less than 2 decades earlier. The square now marks "Kilómetro Zero," the point from which distances on all national highways leading out from Buenos Aires are measured.

Retiro to Recoleta

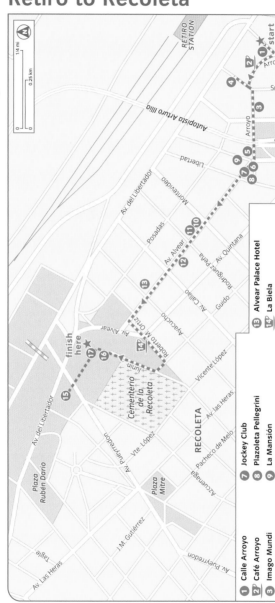

RETIRO STATION

start here

RETIRO

Arroyo

Suipacha

Juncal

Autopista Arturo Illia

Av. 9 de Julio

Arroyo

Libertad

Av. del Libertador

Montevideo

Posadas

Av. Alvear

Av. Quintana

Rodríguez Peña

Guido

Ayacucho

Av. Callao

Roberto M. Ortiz

Vicente López

RECOLETA

Av. las Heras

Pacheco de Melo

Azcuénaga

finish here

Av. Alvear

Junín

Cementerio de la Recoleta

Vte. López

Av. del Libertador

Av. Pueyrredón

Plaza Rubén Darío

Plaza Mitre

J. M. Gutiérrez

Av. Las Heras

Tagle

Av. Pueyrredón

¼ mi
0.25 km

This walking tour takes in Buenos Aires's most elegant streets, from the art galleries of Retiro to Recoleta's Avenida Alvear, a stretch of opulent French-style palaces harking back to the golden age in Buenos Aires and today still home to some of the city's highest-priced real estate and shopping. START: **Taxi to Calle Arroyo (Retiro) or subte to San Martin (C).**

1 ★★ **Calle Arroyo.** This small, winding, tree-lined street at the edge of Retiro may not be in Recoleta proper, but it sure feels like it is. It's one of the city's most elegant thoroughfares, with some of its finest art galleries, antiques shops, and the chic Sofitel hotel, which incorporated the Art Deco 1929 Bencich tower. In 1992, the street was rocked by a bombing that destroyed the Israeli embassy, at the corner of Suipacha. *Between Juncal and Cerrito.*

2 **Café Arroyo.** Part of the luxurious Sofitel Hotel, this traditional cafe is a good stop for coffee and croissants, as well as sandwiches and salads, or full afternoon tea service. If you're more in the mind for a sophisticated cocktail, pop into the swank Bibliotheque lounge. *Arroyo 849.* ☎ *11/ 4131-0001. $.*

Calle Arroyo is one of the city's most elegant thoroughfares.

3 **Imago Mundi.** At Arroyo 971, this inviting bookstore looks like a collector's richly appointed library; it specializes in rare antique editions from the 16th to 19th centuries. *Arroyo 971.*

4 ★ **Museo Fernández Blanco.** A block off Arroyo is this elegant museum occupying a neo-Colonial mansion, the Palacio Noel. It's worth a look to see some splendid colonial decorative art from the Americas, including one of the most important collections of South American colonial silverware. ⏱ *45 min. Suipacha 1442.* ☎ *11/4327-0272. Free admission; donations accepted. Tues–Sun 2–7pm. Subte: San Martin (C).*

5 **Plaza Cataluña.** Across the 16 lanes of traffic on Av. 9 de Julio is this small, quiet plaza named for the semiautonomous region of Spain (of which Barcelona is the capital). In the center is a replica of the Font de Canaletes, the distinctive fountain on La Rambla that is supposed to convert anyone who drinks from it into a lifelong resident of Barcelona. *Arroyo at Av. 9 de Julio.*

6 ★★ **Embajada de Francia.** Across the street from Plaza Cataluña and the beginning of storied Av. Alvear is the French Embassy, in a stunning 1912 Belle Epoque building. Incredibly, this handsome, domed landmark was due to be destroyed, a victim of the impending widening of Av. 9 de Julio in the 1960s, but the French government refused to surrender it. *Cerrito 1399.*

The French Embassy is housed in a stunning 1912 Belle Epoque building.

7 **Jockey Club.** This storied elite social club was founded in 1882 by Carlos Pellegrini (1846–1906), but only moved to this location, the Uzué de Casares mansion, in 1966 when the original on Calle Florida was burned to the ground during a Peronista–working class riot in 1953. *Av. Alvear 1345.*

8 ★ **Plazoleta Pellegrini.** The lovely and quiet small square is perhaps Buenos Aires's finest impersonation of Paris. In the center is a statue of Carlos Pellegrini, who was president of Argentina between

Plaza Francia is a great place to relax next to century-old ombú bushes.

1890 and 1892. The other grand building on the square (on Calle Arroyo) is the ornate **Brazilian Embassy,** like the French Embassy, a former private residence. *Cerrito at Alvear.*

9 ★ **La Mansión.** Just around the corner, down a small stretch of Calle Cerrito, this opulent 1916 French-style mansion was purchased and converted by the Four Seasons Hotel. This adjunct palace, with just seven elegant suites, is where international celebrities like Madonna (who rehearsed her *Evita* balcony scenes here) and the Rolling Stones have stayed. *Cerrito at Posadas.*

10 ★ **La Nunciatore Apostólica.** At no. 1637 on Av. Alvear is this richly ornamental French-style mansion, built in the early 1920s for the Anchorena family, who never lived here. The Cardinal Eugenio Pacelli (1876–1958), who would later become Pope Pius XII, lived here briefly in 1934. The residence was later donated to the Vatican to function as its Apostolic Nunciatore, home to the Vatican's local representative. Pope John Paul II (1920–2005) stayed here on visits to the city in the 1980s. *Av. Alvear 1637.*

11 ★★ **Palacio Duhau.** Next door to the Vatican's representative is a magnificent 1934 palace, modeled on a French castle and the former residence of the Duhau family. It was recently converted into a luxurious Park Hyatt Hotel, one of the most sumptuous in the city. *Av. Alvear 1661.*

12 **Ralph Lauren Polo/Emporio Armani.** Two of the most elegant stores on an avenue full of them—Av. Alvear is the city's version of Beverly Hills' Rodeo Drive—are less noteworthy for their wares than the buildings the shops now inhabit. The Polo store occupies a three-story French chateaux–styled palace, well worth a look inside. *Av. Alvear 1750/1780.*

13 ★★ **Alvear Palace Hotel.** An imposing French neo-Classical building, the Alvear Palace, inaugurated in 1932, has been the longtime standard bearer for luxury hotels in Buenos Aires. While it's prohibitively expensive for most to stay here, there's nothing preventing the rest of us from having a drink at the fabulous Old World bar just off the lobby. *Av. Alvear 1883.*

The Buenos Aires Design Center is full of shops and cafes with outdoor terraces.

14 ★★ **La Biela.** A famous, European-style cafe dating to the 19th century, La Biela is the redoubt of Recoleta's elite, and the umbrella-clad terrace is one of the city's top spots for people-watching. *Quintana 600.* ☎ *11/4804-4135. $$$.*

15 ★ **Plaza Francia.** This square, which hosts an enjoyable weekend arts-and-crafts fair, is a favorite of local families. You can hardly miss the behemoth, century-old *ombú* bushes—native to the pampas and long associated with gaucho culture—and their massive, gnarled roots, wide canopies that can reach 15 meters (49 ft.). *Av. Pueyrredón at Av. Libertador.*

16 ★ **Centro Cultural Recoleta.** If you've already visited Recoleta Cemetery and the colonial church Nuestra Señora de Belén next door (if not, see bullet tk and

bullet **3**, p 28), peek in at this cultural center, which hosts an excellent array of art exhibitions, and theatrical and musical performances. *Junín 1930.* ☎ *11/4803-1040. http://centroculturalrecoleta. org. Free admission. Mon–Fri 2–9pm; Sat–Sun 10am–9pm.*

17 ★ **Buenos Aires Design Center.** A good place to wind up after a long walk through Recoleta is this attention-getting mall, lined with classical statuettes under the church façade of the Cultural Center and done up in bold primary colors. It's full of home-design shops, but just as notable is the long row of cafes and restaurants, with outdoor terraces. *Av. Puerreydón 2501.* ☎ *11/5777-6000. www.design recoleta.com.ar. Subte: No access.*

Art Night

One of the best times to experience Calle Arroyo and Av. Alvear is on "Gallery Night," the last Friday of every month. Several dozen art galleries and antiques dealers open their doors in the evening and celebrate with live classical music, artists on hand to explain their work, and sparkling wine.

San Telmo

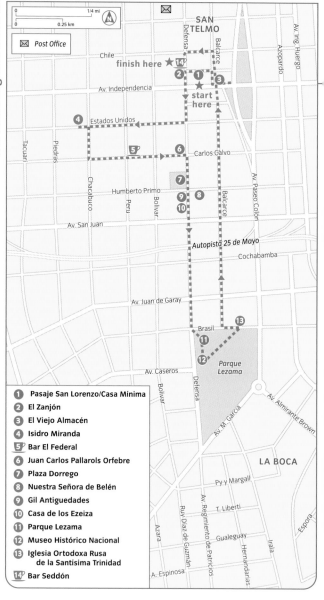

0   1/4 mi
0   0.25 km

⊠ Post Office

1   Pasaje San Lorenzo/Casa Mínima
2   El Zanjón
3   El Viejo Almacén
4   Isidro Miranda
5   Bar El Federal
6   Juan Carlos Pallarols Orfebre
7   Plaza Dorrego
8   Nuestra Señora de Belén
9   Gil Antiguedades
10   Casa de los Ezeiza
11   Parque Lezama
12   Museo Histórico Nacional
13   Iglesia Ortodoxa Rusa
      de la Santísima Trinidad
14   Bar Seddón

San Telmo is, by most accounts, the oldest neighborhood in Buenos Aires. Its cobblestoned streets, old bars, colonial buildings, and faded elegance lend it an authentic, bohemian look. The district is home not just to a lively Sunday Antiques Fair, but a burgeoning art scene and trendy new hotels, restaurants, and clubs; it's also becoming the epicenter of gay life in Buenos Aires. START: **Taxi to Av. Paseo Colón (at San Lorenzo) or subte to Independencia (C).**

1 ★ **Pasaje San Lorenzo.** This cobblestoned street is full of large old *casonas* (mansions), as well as **Casa Mínima** (no. 380), one of the tiniest houses in the city—just 2.5 meters (8¼ ft.) across and 12 meters (39 ft.) deep. Legend holds that it was built by a freed slave (whose former owner allowed him to build on his property) after the abolition of slavery in 1812, though the reality may be less romantic, simply the result of a subdivided property. *Between Defensa & Av. Paseo Colón.*

2 ★★ kids **El Zanjón.** A meticulously restored 1830 mansion is less notable for what's above ground than what lies underneath: vast tunnels, part of a network that once ran beneath large sections of Buenos Aires, channeling water from the river. See portions of the original foundations and brick vaults on guided visits. *See bullet* **4**, *p 28.*

3 ★ **El Viejo Almacén.** This colonial-style 1798 building was once a general store and then the British Hospital. Since it was acquired by the tango singer Edmundo Rivero (1911–1986) in 1969, it has been at the forefront of San Telmo's association with tango, as well as the neighborhood's economic revival. Dinner tango shows are perhaps slicker than what one might expect from the neighborhood, but still enjoyable and more intimate than at large *tanguerías*. *Independencia 300, San Telmo.* ☎ *11/4307-7388. Subte: Independencia (C).*

The cobblestoned streets of Pasaje San Lorenzo.

4 ★ **Isidro Miranda.** To get a taste of San Telmo's artistic side, visit one of the neighborhood's hip art galleries, which tend to be much more contemporary than what you'll find in upscale Recoleta. This clean, two-level space presents interesting installations, photography, sculpture, and painting from both established and young artists, both Argentine and international. *Estados Unidos 726.* ☎ *11/4361-4034. Subte: Independencia (C).*

5 ★★★ **Bar El Federal.** An erstwhile grocer from 1864, with a stunning original carved-wood bar and antique cash registers, it's a mandatory stop in the neighborhood, whether it's for a coffee and the newspaper or a good-value lunch of picadas. *Carlos Calvo 599.* ☎ *11/4300-4313. $.*

El Viejo Almacén is at the forefront of San Telmo's tango scene.

6 ★★★ **Juan Carlos Pallarols Orfebre.** Home to one of the most prestigious master silversmiths, not only in Buenos Aires, but anywhere on the planet. Pallarols has made exquisite silver gifts for everyone from Pope John Paul II and the King of Spain to Lady Di and Antonio Banderas. Many of his (understandably expensive) pieces have a distinct *criolla* flavor. *Defensa 1039.* ☎ *11/4300-6555. www.pallarols. com.ar. Subte: Independencia (C).*

7 ★★★ **kids Plaza Dorrego.** The heart of San Telmo, the second-oldest square in the city, is best known for its Sunday antiques fair, not just for the shopping, but also the stellar street performers and overflowing bars and cafes. *See bullet* **5**, *p 16.*

8 ★ **Nuestra Señora de Belén.** An 18th-century Jesuit church known to many locals as Templo de San Pedro Telmo is a mix of colonial, neo-Classical, and Baroque elements. *See bullet* **3**, *p 28.*

9 ★★ **Gil Antiguedades.** This eclectic antiques dealer, specializing in vintage clothing, is one of the most interesting in San Telmo. You'll find a diverse array of more than 6,000 antique items, including gaucho-style ponchos, Victorian dresses, rugs, and antique lace. *Humberto 1° 412.* ☎ *11/4361-5019. www.gilantiguedades.com.ar. Subte: Independencia (C).*

10 ★ **Casa de los Ezeiza.** When the rich ruled San Telmo, they lived in grand homes like this, which later became a *conventillo,* or multi-family tenement house. Also called

Juan Carlos Pallarols Orfebre is a master silversmith who has made gifts for Lady Diana and the Pope.

Pasaje de La Defensa, it was converted into a school and warehouse before being repurposed to accommodate the San Telmo antiques phenomenon. Today, it's a picturesque two-story, open-air market with multiple vendors around two interior patios. *See bullet* 6, *p 17.*

11 **Parque Lezama.** This park—yet another of the city's tree-rich green spaces designed by Frenchman Carlos Thays, in 1891—is on the spot where Buenos Aires is said to have been originally settled by Pedro de Mendoza (c. 1487–1537) in 1536 (the settlement was soon abandoned, and the city's permanent founding didn't come until 1580). It was later the site of a slave trading company. Despite the park's Greek statues and Parisian fountain, it's a bit unkempt and shabby around the edges. *AV. Brasil at Defensa.*

12 ★ **Museo Histórico Nacional.** The National History Museum—in existence since 1889—occupies a colonial mansion that belonged to the powerful Lezama family. *See bullet* 1, *p 27.*

13 ★ **Iglesia Ortodoxa Rusa de la Santísima Trinidad.** The bulbous, bright-blue Byzantine cupolas atop this 1904 Russian Orthodox church are an unexpected sight in San Telmo. The church was

Bar Seddon is perfect for an evening cocktail.

inspired by 17th-century Moscovite churches (and funded in part by donations solicited in Russia). *Brasil 315, San Telmo.*

14 ★★★ **Bar Seddon.** Finish up the day back near where you began, at this atmospheric spot that's perfect for an evening cocktail. A refurbished 19th-century pharmacy, it incorporates antique train mirrors and bits of old bars from across the city. In the evenings, there are live blues, jazz, and tango performances. *Defensa 695 (at Chile).* ☎ *11/4342-3700. $$.*

San Telmo's Evolution

San Telmo, the birthplace of Buenos Aires, has been through several incarnations, evolving from a 19th-century elite residential neighborhood of aristocratic families and palatial residences to a rough-and-tumble district of *conventillos* (multi-family tenements). It slid further into disrepute during the second half of the 20th century, but new restaurants, hotels, art galleries, and clubs have spearheaded its ongoing transformation into today's fashionable, if still slightly scruffy, district.

Palermo Chico

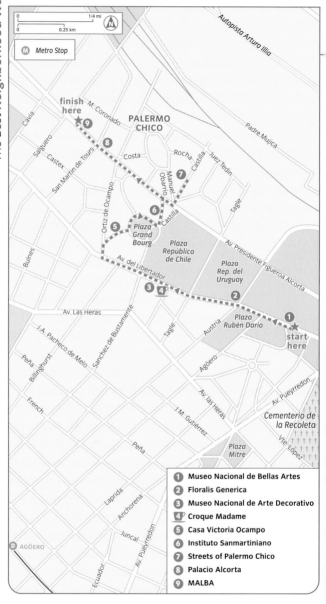

0 _____ 1/4 mi
0 _____ 0.25 km

Ⓜ Metro Stop

Autopista Arturo Illia

finish here ★ ❾ M. Coronado

PALERMO CHICO

Padre Mujica

Cavia
Salguero
Castex
San Martin de Tours
Costa
Rocha
Castilla
Juez Tedin
Manuel Obario
❼
❽
Tagle
Ortiz de Ocampo
Castilla
❻
❺ Plaza Grand Bourg
Plaza República de Chile
Av. Presidente Figueroa Alcorta
Bulnes
Av. del Libertador
Plaza Rep. del Uruguay
❸ ❹
❷
Av. Las Heras
J.A. Pacheco de Melo
Sánchez de Bustamante
Tagle
Austria
Plaza Rubén Dario
❶ ★ **start here**

Peña
Billinghurst
French
Agüero
Av. las Heras
J.M. Gutiérrez
Av. Pueyrredon
Cementerio de la Recoleta
Vte. López

Peña
Plaza Mitre

Laprida
Anchorena
Juncal
Av. Pueyrredon
Ⓓ AGÜERO
Ecuador

This quiet and exclusive residential district is perhaps the most elegant in Buenos Aires. Full of stately mansions and embassies, it is also home to manicured gardens by Carlos Thays, the city's preeminent landscape architect at the turn of the 20th century. START: **Taxi to Av. del Libertador (at Libres del Sur).**

① ★★ Museo Nacional de Bellas Artes. A few blocks from the heart of Palermo Chico, Argentina's most important art museum, with its imposing red columns, looks nothing like its former incarnation, when it was the pump station for the city's water supply, prior to its transformation in 1933. *See bullet ⑤, p 57.*

② ★ kids Floralis Generica. In the midst of Plaza de las Naciones Unidas, Eduardo Catalano's (1917–) massive, 20-meter-high (66-ft.-high) steel-and-aluminum sculpture of a "generic flower" opens electronically at the beginning of each day and closes at sunset (although 4 days a year, it remains open: May 25, Sept 21, and Dec 24 and 25). *Av. Figueroa Alcorta at Austria.*

③ ★★ Museo Nacional de Arte Decorativo. Otherwise known as Palacio Errázuriz, this French-style 1918 mansion is grand in every way; inside, it displays the Eurocentric art collection of its former owners, who donated the house and its contents to the state. *See bullet ①, p 21.*

④ ★ Croque Madame. On the premises of the Museo de Arte Decorativo, this great cafe-restaurant has a terrific shaded outdoor terrace, a world removed from the hubbub of Av. Libertador. While I can never resist a coffee here, it also makes a perfect stop for a relaxed lunch or dinner. *See bullet ②, p 21.*

The steel and aluminum "generic flower" statue is becoming an emblem of the city.

Croque Madame is part of the Museo de Arte Decorativo.

⑤ ★ Casa Victoria Ocampo.

Most of Palermo Chico's mansions are elegant, turn-of-the-20th-century buildings that would look at home in Paris. This all-white modernist 1929 home, which belonged to a prominent literary figure, Victoria Ocampo (1890–1979), looks more like Miami Beach. It now houses the Fondo de las Artes, a contemporary art foundation. *See bullet ③, p 46.*

⑥ Instituto Sanmartiniano.

This 1933 institute is an exact replica of the house where General José de San Martín (1778–1850), known as the "Father of the Argentine Nation," lived in Grand Bourg, France from 1834 to 1848. Latin American history buffs will find archives related to the life of "El Libertador." *Mariscal Castilla (at Alejandro Aguado).* ☎ *11/4801-0848. www.sanmartiniano.gov.ar.*

⑦ ★★ Streets of Palermo Chico.

Looking and feeling like a village within the city, the delightful, verdant streets of this elite neighborhood (which spills across either side of Av. Alcorta) are lined with chateaux, embassies, fragrant vegetation, and tall trees. Though most of the homes are tucked behind high iron gates, you're free to stroll along the streets Ortiz de Ocampo, Aguado, Obarrio, Ombú, and Castilla, marveling at how quiet and isolated from the big city they seem. *Between Tagle & Salguero.*

⑧ Palacio Alcorta.

Architecture fans will appreciate this 1927 apartment building, designed by the Italian architect Mario Palanti, who was responsible for one of Buenos Aires's most distinctive buildings, Palacio Barolo (see p 12). *Av. Figueroa Alcorta 3399.*

⑨ ★★ MALBA.

Local businessman Eduardo Costantini's extensive private collection constitutes the Museo de Arte Latinoamericano de Buenos Aires. Major contemporary and modern Latin American artists include Diego Rivera (1886–1957), Frida Kahlo (1907–1954), Roberto Matta (1911–2002), and Wilfredo Lam (1902–1982), as well the Argentines Antonio Berni (1905–1981) and Xul Solar (1887–1963). *See bullet ③, p 22.* ●

Casa Victoria Ocampo houses a contemporary art foundation.

Shopping Best Bets

Best Place for **Victorian Nightgowns**
★★ Gil Antiguedades, *Humberto 1° 412 (p 79)*

Best Place for **Dressing Like a Gaucho**
★★ Arandú, *Paraguay 1259 (p 81)*

Best Place for **Furry Purses**
★★ Pasión Argentina, *Ravignani 1780 (p 84)*

Best **Theatrical Bookstore**
★★★ El Ateneo Grand Splendid, *Av. Santa Fe 1860 (p 80)*

Best Place for **Mens Clothing**
★★ Balthazar, *Gorriti 5131 (p 80)*

Best Place for **Antiques**
★★★ San Telmo Feria de Antiguedades, *Plaza Dorrego (p 85)*

Best **Impersonation of Carrie Bradshaw's Closet**
★★★ Lucila Iotti, *Malabia 2212 (p 84)*

Best **Non-Hotel Day Spa**
★★ Ser Agua Club & Spa, *Blvd. Cerviño 3626 (p 85)*

Best Place for **Creative Leather Goods**
★★★ Humawaca, *El Salvador 4692 (p 84)*

Best **Wine Cellar**
★★ Terroir, *Buschiazzo 3040 (p 86)*

Best Place for **Female Fashionistas**
★★ Trosman, *Posadas 1245 (p 81)*

Best Place for **Silver Knives and Frames Fit for a King**
★★★ Juan Carlos Pallarols Orfebre, *Defensa 1039 (p 83)*

Best Place for **Tango Vixens**
★★★ Comme Il Faut, *1239 Arenales, Apt. M (2nd floor) (p 86)*

Best Place for **Girly Dresses Amelie Might Wear**
★ Las Oreiro, *4780 Honduras (p 81)*

Best Place for **Outfitting Your New Estancia**
★★★ airedelsur, *Av. Alvear 1883 (p 81)*

Best Place for **Junk That's Anything But**
★ Mercado de las Pulgas, *Niceto Vega 200 block (p 85)*

Best Place for **Chic Everyday Handbags**
★★ Prüne, *Florida 96 (p 84)*;
★★ Qara, *Gurruchaga 1548 (p 85)*

Best Place for **Lingering Over a Book**
★★ Boutique del Libro, *Thames 1762 (p 79)*

Florentina Muraña has unique leather bags at reasonable prices.

Centro/San Telmo Shopping

aireдelsur **4**
Almacén de Tangos
Generales **28**
The Antique Book Shop **8**
Arandú **3**
Buenos Aires Design **2**
Casa López **11**
Comme Il Faut **7**
Feria de Plaza Francia **1**
Flabella **18**
Galeria Ruth Benzacar **10**
Galerías Pacífico **15**
Gil Antiguedades **27**
Isidro Miranda **20**
Juan Carlos Pallarols
Orfebre **25**
La Casa del Habano **13**
Laguanacazul **22**
Patio Bullrich **6**
Plata Nativa **14**
Prüne **12**

Rossi & Carusso **5**
San Telmo Feria de
Antiguedades **26**
Silvia Petroccia Antiguedades **24**
Tango Mina Dancewear **17**

Tango Moda **19**
30quarenta **9**
Trosman **16**
Un Lugar En El Mundo **23**
Walrus Books **21**

Previous page: Brightly colored tapestries on display at Arte Étnico Argentino in Palermo Soho.

Palermo Shopping

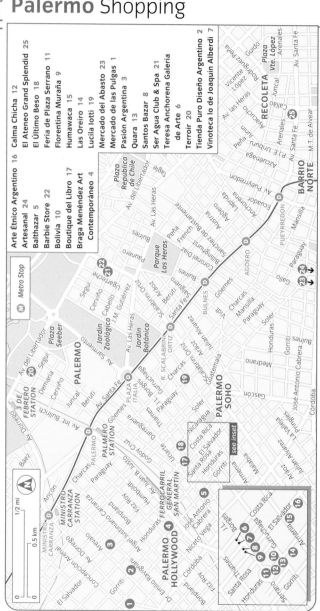

Shopping A to Z

Antiques & Art

★★ Braga Menéndez Art Contemporáneo PALERMO HOLLYWOOD Florencia Braga Menéndez's gallery is one of the top spaces in the city for contemporary art. She works with about three dozen young and established Argentine artists. *Humboldt 1574.* ☎ *11/4775-5577. www. galeriabm.com. AE, MC, V. Subte: No access. Map p 78.*

★★ Galeria Ruth Benzacar RETIRO One of the city's most prestigious art galleries—which exhibits at major fairs in Europe and North America—is tucked underground at the beginning of Calle Florida. Featured artists include some of the biggest contemporary names in the Argentine art world. *Florida 1000, Retiro.* ☎ *11/4313-8480. AE, MC, V. www. ruthbenzacar.com. Subte: San Martín (C). Map p 77.*

★★ Gil Antiguedades SAN TELMO One of San Telmo's best-known antiques shops, a specialist in vintage clothing, including Victorian dresses and antique lace. *Humberto 1° 412, San Telmo.* ☎ *11/4361-5019. www.gilantiguedades.com.ar. AE, DC, MC, V. Subte: Independencia. Map p 77.*

★ Isidro Miranda SAN TELMO This two-level space presents interesting installations, photography, sculpture, and painting from established and young artists, both Argentine and international. *Estados Unidos 726.* ☎ *11/4361-4034. www. isidromiranda.com.ar. MC, V. Subte: Independencia (C). Map p 77.*

★ Silvia Petroccia Antiguedades SAN TELMO An antiques shop with an eclectic array of wares, including mirrors and chandeliers, many of them one-of-a-kind pieces. *Defensa 1002.* ☎ *11/4362-0156. MC,*

V. Subte: Independencia (C). Map p 77.

★ Teresa Anchorena Galeria de Arte PALERMO SOHO A sophisticated and friendly art gallery, featuring contemporary Argentine artists, such as El Chaco's Milo Lockett, as well as nicely selected mid-century modern furnishings. *Costa Rica 4818.* ☎ *11/4831-9828. AE, MC, V. Subte: No access. Map p 78.*

Books

The Antique Book Shop BARRIO NORTE A specialist in rare books, antique manuscripts, and maps, with a focus on Argentine and gaucho themes. *Libertad 1236.* ☎ *11-4815-0658. MC, V. Subte: Uruguay (B). Map p 77.*

★★ Boutique del Libro PALERMO SOHO While the English-language section, coffee-table books, and tall stacks with ladders are the main attractions, I'm partial to the attached cafe, with Wi-Fi and

The café at Boutique del Libro is a great spot for quick Internet access and tasty snacks.

The atmosphere at Balthazar's is as elegant as the clothing.

good snacks and drinks. *Thames 1762.* ☎ *11/4833-6637. www. boutiquedellibro.com.ar. MC, V. Subte: Independencia (C). Map p 78.*

★★★ El Ateneo Grand Splendid BARRIO NORTE
An incredible experience for a bookstore, in a grand 1919 movie theater, with rows of books occupying three levels that were once box seats and a great cafe on the former stage. *Av. Santa Fe 1860.* ☎ *11/4811-6104.*

Bolivia has hip casual wear for men.

AE, DC, MC, V. Subte: Callo (B). Map p 78.

★ Walrus Books SAN TELMO
A good little book shop with gently used books in English, as well as Latin American literature and non-fiction in translation. *Estados Unidos 617.* ☎ *11/4300-7135. www.walrus-books.com.ar. AE, DC, MC, V. Subte: Independencia (C). Map p 77.*

Cigars
La Casa del Habano CENTRO
The place to get your hands on a Cuban—cigar, that is—while in Buenos Aires. *Paraguay 658.* ☎ *11/4313-4844. www.lacasadelhabano.com. MC, V. Subte: San Martin (C). Map p 77.*

Fashion
★★ Balthazar PALERMO SOHO
You'll need to ring the doorbell to be let in here, one of the swankest and best-looking men's shops in town, something akin to the Argentine Paul Smith. *Gorriti 5131. (Second location at Defensa 1008, San Telmo.)* ☎ *11/4834-6235. www. balthazarshop.com. AE, DC, MC, V. Subte: No access. Map p 78.*

kids Barbie Store PALERMO
South America's first store dedicated to Barbie has outfits for dolls, and a cafe and beauty parlor for Barbie fans. *Scalabrini Ortiz 3170.* ☎ *0810/4444-BARBIE. www.barbie-stores.com. AE, DC, MC, V. Subte: Plaza Italia (D). Map p 78.*

Bolivia PALERMO SOHO
Hipster dudes will love the rock 'n roll t-shirts and military jackets at this self-consciously cool boutique in a Palermo townhouse. *Gurruchaga 1581.* ☎ *11/4832-6284. www.bolivia online.com.ar. AE, MC, V. Subte: No access. Map p 78.*

★ El Último Beso PALERMO

SOHO   An inviting, shabby-chic, and feminine shop with a nice assortment of women's elegant fashions, along with home-decor accents, and a sweet little cafe and inviting restaurant in back. *Nicaragua 4880.* ☎ *11/4832-771. www. elultimobeso.com.ar. MC, V. Subte: No access. Map p 78.*

★ Las Oreiro PALERMO SOHO

The Argentine singer, model, and actress Natalia Oreiro owns this whimsical boutique bursting with colorful and girlish fashions. There's a retro-inspired pop sensibility, something like the French film *Amelie*, about the place and the designs. *4780 Honduras.* ☎ *11/4834-6161. MC, V. Subte: No access. Map p 78.*

★★ Trosman RECOLETA   A

young, cutting-edge designer, Jessica Trosman's gauzy, exotic dresses and sheer tops have a great urban sense of style and have won notice in Argentina and retail presence in Paris and Tokyo. *Galerías Pacífico & Patio Bullrich (see "Malls").* ☎ *11/5555-5344 or 11/4814-7411. AE, DC, MC, V. Subte: San Martín (C). Map p 77.*

★★ Un Lugar En El Mundo SAN

TELMO   Named after a memorable Argentine movie, this hip shop features rising young designers and their cool duds for both men and women, many with unique prints, as well as some unexpected accessories. *Defensa 891.* ☎ *11/4362-3836. DC, MC, V. Subte: Independencia (C). Map p 77.*

Gaucho/Polo/Argentine Style

★★★ airedelsur RECOLETA

Exquisite handcrafted home decor items, including trays, candelabras, lamps of bone, alpaca silver, and leather, all with a rustic-chic, very Argentine look. Also, fashion accessories, such as belts and handbags. The high-end North American department stores Barneys and Neiman Marcus carry their items. *Av. Alvear 1883.* ☎ *11/4803-6100. www.airedelsur.com. AE, DC, MC, V. Subte: No access. Map p 77.*

★★ Arandú PALERMO SOHO

This shop has macho upper-class Argentina written all over it: sheepskin and suede jackets, beautiful polo riding boots, saddles, hats,

El Último Beso is an inviting women's shop with a café in the back.

PRIME SHOPPING ZONES

In two prominent Buenos Aires barrios, shopping is an attraction for visitors that nearly surpasses all others: **Recoleta,** known for its high-end shops (especially along Av. Alvear), and trendy **Palermo Viejo** (particularly Palermo Soho), with its hipper boutiques, younger fashion designers, and art galleries. **San Telmo,** famed for its Sunday market, is the city's antiquing destination *par excellence.* In recent years, **Barrio Norte** has emerged as a cool new retail area, especially for home furnishings. The traditional shopping destination, pedestrian-only **Calle Florida,** has lost a step, though it still draws crowds to the Beaux Arts mall Galerías Pacífico. For **outlet shopping** in Palermo Viejo, head to Av. Córdoba (between Scalabrini Ortiz and Godoy Cruz). There (or very nearby), you'll find fashion outlets such as Cardón, Lacoste, Chocolate, Yves St. Laurent, Quicksilver, and Prüne.

mates, and leather sports bags, as well as other polo and equestrian items. *Paraguay 1259. (Second location at Ayacucho 1924, Recoleta.)* ☎ *11/4816-3689 or 11/4800-1575. www.arandu.com.ar. AE, MC, V. Subte: No access. Map p 77.*

★★★ Arte Étnico Argentino PALERMO
SOHO   A beautiful shop, with a constellation of chairs dangling from the ceiling, featuring rich tapestries and wool rugs (many with a modern design aesthetic) from northern Argentina, as well as rustic hand-crafted furnishings. *El Salvador 4600.* ☎ *11/4833-6661. www.arte etnicoargentino.com. MC, V. Subte: No access. Map p 78.*

Home Decor & Furnishings
★ Calma Chicha PALERMO SOHO
A funky, fun shop with playful household items, such as *pingüinos* (penguin-shaped wine jugs, originally from the 1960s), as well as

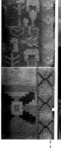

Arte Étnico Argentino carries rugs and tapestries from northern Argentina.

large cowhides and ultra-soft sheepskin rugs. *Honduras 4925.* ☎ *11/4831-1818. www. calmachicha.com. AE, DC, MC, V. Subte: No access. Map p 78.*

★ Laguanacazul
SAN TELMO   An art gallery and shop with original items—both decorative and functional, including clothing—by artists and artisans, all artfully displayed on a long wall of floor-to-ceiling shelves. *Defensa 677.* ☎ *11/4342-9863. MC, V. Subte: Independencia (C). Map p 77.*

★★ Santos Bazar PALERMO
SOHO   This small corner shop has a stylish selection of alpaca silver and horn trays, servers, candlesticks, knives, and other items, perfect for gifts with an Argentine accent. *Thames 1759.* ☎ *11/4883-3770. www.santosbazar.com.ar. MC, V. Subte: No access. Map p 78.*

★★★ Tienda Puro Diseño
Argentino PALERMO SOHO This high-end design shop features items by more than 100 Argentine designers. Items are mostly home design (with some funky stuff, such as tables made from old TV sets), though you'll also find jewelry and leather accessories. *Gorriti 5953.* ☎ *11/4776-8037. www.purodiseno. com.ar. AE, MC, V. Subte: No access. Map p 78.*

30quarenta RETIRO A vibrantly colored shop among the chic art galleries of Calle Arroyo, this place has cool retro advertising and film posters, imaginative lamps, and fun items like Carlos Gardel bowling pins. *Arroyo 890.* ☎ *11/4326-1065. www.30quarenta.com. Subte: San Martin (C). Map p 77.*

Jewelry & Silver
★★★ Juan Carlos Pallarols
Orfebre SAN TELMO The retail outlet for a world-renowned silversmith who has fashioned stunning silverware, frames, ornate candlesticks, and steak knives for the rich and famous, including royalty. *Defensa 1039.* ☎ *11/4300-6555. www.pallarols. com.ar. AE, MC, V. Subte: Independencia (C). Map p 77.*

30quarenta offers fun retro accessories and prints.

Santos Bazar has stylish Argentinian gifts such as alpaca silver.

★★ Plata Nativa CENTRO Fash-
ionistas flock to this little shop, hidden away in an arcade, for stylish ethnic Argentine pieces, made with silver and colorful textiles. You'll also find antique folk art, including South American weavings, religious paintings, altarpieces, and colonial- and gaucho-style silver items. *Galería del Sol, Florida 860.* ☎ *11/ 4312-1398. www.platanativa.com. AE, MC, V. Subte: San Martin (C). Map p 77.*

Leather Goods & Shoes
Casa López RETIRO This very traditional shop isn't the most exciting and certainly isn't cutting-edge, but it specializes in well-made Argentine leather products, from suede jackets to classic handbags. *Marcelo T. de Alvear 640/658, Centro.* ☎ *11/4311-3044. www.casa lopez.com.ar. MC, V. Subte: San Martin. Map p 77.*

★ Florentina Muraña PALERMO
SOHO A great selection of affordable bags, shoes, and leather

accessories (for men and women), many in bright colors or with spots and furry cowhides, can be found at this amiable corner shop. *Borges 1760.* ☎ *11/4833-4137. www. florentinamurania.com.ar. MC, V. Subte: No access. Map p 78.*

★★★ Humawaca PALERMO
SOHO This is among the chicest (and most expensive) leather brands in Buenos Aires, with "art bags," like circular leather handbags, butterfly-shaped BKP backpacks, and sleek clutches. *El Salvador 4692. (Other branches at Posadas 1380, Recoleta; & Galerías Pacífico.)* ☎ *11/4832-2662. www.humawaca.com. AE, DC, MC, V. Subte: No access. Map p 78.*

★★★ Lucila Iotti PALERMO
SOHO There's little like Lucila's distinctive shoe and boot designs. Strong, quirky, and boldly colored, these aren't for every woman, but many young women will be in heaven. *Malabia 2212.* ☎ *11/4833-0206. www.lucilaiotti.com. AE, DC, MC, V. Subte: No access. Map p 78.*

★ Pasión Argentina PALERMO
HOLLYWOOD The elegant and stylish cowhide eyeglass cases, coin purses, belts, and oversized bags

Florentina Murana has a good selection of chic shoes, bags, and accessories.

found here—a Fair Trade shop and factory—combine a modern aesthetic with the traditional artisanry of indigenous communities in Chaco (northern Argentina). *Ravignani 1780.* ☎ *11/4777-7550. www. pasion-argentina.com.ar. AE, V. Subte: No access. Map p 78.*

★★ Prüne RETIRO My wife's favorite chain, hands-down, for stylish and luxurious handbags (and shoes). Given their quality and design, they're fairly priced and always (much to my horror) have something new. *Florida 963. (About a dozen other branches, including at Gorriti 4812, Palermo Soho; & an outlet at Gurruchaga 861.)* ☎ *11/4893-2634. www.prune.com. ar. AE, MC, V. Subte: No access. Map p 77.*

★★ Qara PALERMO SOHO The
name means "leather" in Quechua, so you know what you'll find here. A young American designer opened this handsome shop with well-crafted handbags and satchels for men and has made her mark in Argentine leather goods. *Gurruchaga 1548.* ☎ *11/4834-6361. www.qara.com. AE, MC, V. Subte: No access. Map p 78.*

★ Rossi & Caruso RECOLETA
A classic shop, around since 1941, that has outfitted Prince Philip of England and the king and queen of Spain with traditional leather goods, including luggage and high-quality purses, wallets, and belts. *Posadas 1387. (Second branch at Av. Santa Fe 1377, Galerías Pacífico.)* ☎ *11/ 4800-1174. www.rossicaruso.com. AE, DC, MC, V. Subte: No access. Map p 77.*

Malls
★★ Mercado del Abasto
ABASTO A famous Art Deco building from the 1930s, converted into a full-scale mall in the late 1990s. In addition to a bevy of shops of all stripes, it houses the Museo de

Niños (Kids' Museum) and a Kosher McDonalds. *Av. Corrientes 3247.* ☎ *11/4959-3400. Subte: Carlos Gardel (B). Map p 78.*

★ **Buenos Aires Design** RECO-LETA Occupying a prime location just steps from Recoleta Cemetery, with outdoor "terraza" cafes and shops concentrating on home design and art. *Av. Puerreydón 2501.* ☎ *11/5777-6000. www. designrecoleta.com.ar. Subte: No access . Map p 77.*

★ **Galerías Pacífico** CENTRO On famed pedestrian-only Calle Florida, more notable for the turn-of-the-20th-century building and dome frescoes than the shops. *Florida 737.* ☎ *11/5555-5100. www.galerias pacifico.com.ar. Subte: Florida (B) or San Martín (C). Map p 77.*

★ **Patio Bullrich** RETIRO A favorite stomping ground of the Porteño elite, in a historic building (once the meat auction house), with chandeliers and a glass ceiling. *Posadas 1245.* ☎ *11/4814-7400. Subte: San Martín. Map p 77.*

Markets
Feria de Plaza Francia RECO-LETA An enjoyable open-air market with touristy gifts and crafts items, popular with families. *See bullet ⑮, p 67.*

★ **Mercado de las Pulgas** PAL-ERMO HOLLYWOOD At the outer reaches of Palermo Viejo, this flea market is where friends of mine outfitted their chick Palermo apartment. From mid-century furnishings to artwork and Venetian-glass chandeliers, this place makes for a fun hunt. *Niceto Vega 200 block (between Dorrego & Concepcion Arenales).*

Feria de Plaza Serrano PALERMO SOHO Artisans gather in front of the bars and cafes in the heart of Palermo Viejo every weekend for a

Abasto Shopping Center is a beautiful Art Deco building, with shops and a children's museum.

street fair of funky t-shirts, jewelry, and hippie accoutrements. *Calle Serrano (at Honduras).*

★★★ **San Telmo Feria de Antiguedades** SAN TELMO The granddaddy of Buenos Aires markets, this antiques fair every Sunday is one of the top tourist attractions in town. *See bullet ⑦, p 70.*

Spas
★★ **Ser Agua Club & Spa** PAL-ERMO A spectacular day spa in an ingeniously converted old Palermo townhouse, painted soothing white and apple green. Great for massages, water treatments, and facials, including full-day beauty and stress-relief programs. *Blvd. Cerviño 3626.* ☎ *11/4807-4688. www.agua clubspa.com. Subte: Plaza Italia (D). Map p 78.*

Tango Specialty Shops
Almacén de Tangos Generales SAN TELMO The place to pick up tango CDs, music scores, and sundry tango-related souvenirs. *Don Anselmo Aieta 1067, at Plaza Dorrego.* ☎ *11/ 4362-7190. MC, V. Subte: Independencia (C). Map p 77.*

The Sunday San Telmo Feria de Antiguedades is one of the top tourist attractions in the city.

★ **Artesanal** ABASTO   Stylish handmade tango shoes made by the celebrated Susana Villarroel. *Anchorena 537.* ☎ *11/4953-6874. MC, V. Subte: Carlos Gardel (B). Map p 78.*

★★★ **Comme Il Faut** RECOLETA Some of the more daring tango-shoe designs seen on dance floors come from this small shop outfitted with leopard-print benches. The materials and designs are sexy and the heels vertiginous. *1239 Arenales, Apt. M (2nd floor).* ☎ *11/4815-5690. MC, V. Subte: No access. Map p 77.*

★ **Flabella** CENTRO   One of the top shops in town for handmade women's and men's tango shoes of unique and flashy designs. Though there are tons to choose from, veteran *tangueros* may want to get theirs custom-made. *Suipacha 263.* ☎ *11/4322-6036. www.flabella.com. MC, V. Subte: Carlos Pellegrini (B). Map p 77.*

★★ **Tango Mina Dancewear** CENTRO   Modern takes on tango fashions, from sexy skirts and dresses to halter tops and hip, swishy pants, these clothes are designed to move with a woman on the dance floor. *Riobamba 486, 10th floor.* ☎ *11/4952-3262. www.tango mina.com.ar. MC, V. Subte: Callao (B). Map p 77.*

★★ **Tango Moda** CENTRO   A visit to this shop is worth it just to get to the top of Palacio Barolo and the rapturous views from the two terraces. But you'll also find a great selection of men's and women's tango clothes and shoes. *Av. de Mayo 1370, 16th floor.* ☎ *11/4381-4049. www.tango moda.com.ar. MC, V. Subte: Sáenz Peña (A). Map p 77.*

WINE

★★ **Terroir** PALERMO   Behind the heavy door of this handsome Palermo town house, it's all about sophistication and selection. There's a tasting room, top-floor sundeck (for occasional *asados*), and library wines (not that easy to find in Argentina). Shipping can be arranged. *Buschiazzo 3040.* ☎ *11/4778-3443. www.terroir. com.ar. AE, MC, V. Subte: No access. Map p 77.*

★★ **Vinoteca lo de Joaquín Alberdi** PALERMO SOHO   A stylish and easygoing, friendly shop that offers special tastings of high-end wines, as well as excellent recommendations that will get you up to speed on Argentina's signature grapes, malbec and torrontés. *Borges 1772.* ☎ *11/4832-5329. www.lodejoaquin alberdi.com.ar. MC, V. Subte: No access. Map p 78.* ●

5 The Great Outdoors

The Great Outdoors

Palermo's Parks & Gardens

1. Parque Carlos Thays
2. Plaza Alemania
3. Jardín Japonés
4. Restaurante del Jardín Japonés
5. Parque Tres de Febrero
6. Los Lagos/Rosedal
7. Jardín Zoológico
8. Jardín Botánico Carlos Thays
9. Parque Las Heras
10. Na Serapia
11. Hipódromo de Palermo
12. Campo Argentino de Polo
13. La Rural

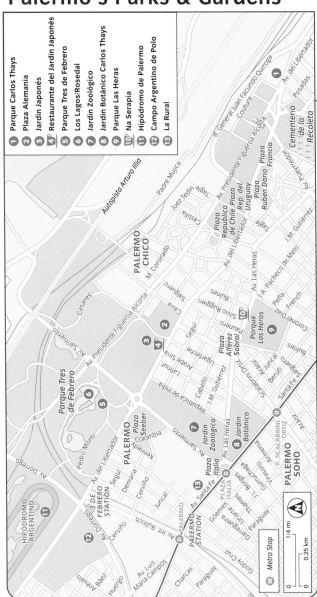

Previous page: Kids feed the koi carp in the lakes at Jardín Japonés.

If the traffic and exhaust in Buenos Aires have you wondering how the city could possibly be named "good airs," you'll see why in Palermo, home to the city's most expansive green spaces and more than than 80 hectares (198 acres) of greenery from Recoleta to Palermo, bordered by Av. Libertador. The early-20th-century French landscape designer Carlos Thays (1839–1934) left his green fingerprints all over the city, but nowhere more so than in Palermo. START: **Taxi to Av. Libertador (at Av. Callao).**

① ★ Parque Carlos Thays. Named for the early-20th-century French landscape designer instrumental in so many of the city's parks, this example at the edge of Recoleta is where an amusement park operated until an accidental death shut it down. Today, there's a massive, muscular torso sculpture by the contemporary Colombian artist Fernando Botero (1932–). *Av. del Libertador (at Av. Callao).*

② Plaza Alemania. This Palermo green space designed by Thays features a small park with a flower garden, inaugurated in 1914. The fountain, *Riqueza Agropecuaria Argentina,* by the sculptor Adolf Bredow (1875–1953), has a decidedly agricultural bent. It was donated by the German community in 1910. *Av. del Libertador (at Scalabrini Ortiz).*

③ ★★ kids Jardín Japonés. Another gift from a community of ex-patriots, these tranquil traditional Japanese gardens were established in 1979. The isolated spot (*AR $5; children ages 6-10 AR $1. Daily 10am–6pm*) is a favorite of families on weekends. Small artificial lakes are stocked with giant koi carp that pester kids to be fed. *Av. Figueroa Alcorta (at Av. Casares). See bullet ⑥, p. 53.*

④ ★★ Restaurante del Jardín Japonés. Within the Japanese Gardens is a peaceful pagoda with a tea house, offering a variety of Asian teas and sweets, and a Japanese restaurant serving soups, sushi, and more. *Av. Figueroa Alcorta (at Av. Casares).* ☎ *11/4800-1322. $$.*

The tranquil Jardín Japonés, a peaceful hideaway donated by Japanese ex-patriots.

Club de Amigos

Although you can join Porteños and run, bicycle, or skate in Parque Tres de Febrero, if you're looking for more facilities and/or formal sports outings, head to the friendly sounding Club de Amigos, which is within the park and has an Olympic-sized pool, tennis courts, and soccer fields, as well as a full gymnasium and fitness classes. Best of all, you don't have to be a member; guests need only pay a reasonable day fee (AR$10) to use all the facilities. Friends who stayed a couple of months in Buenos Aires went every day with their two young daughters. In fact, I think it was their favorite thing about the city. *Av. Figueroa Alcorta 3885, Palermo.* ☎ *11/4801-1213. www.clubdeamigos.org.ar. Subte: Plaza Italia (D).*

⑤ ★★★ kids **Parque Tres de Febrero.** The city's most famous green space is something akin to Buenos Aires's Central Park. Established by presidential decree back in 1872, the park now comprises 405 hectares (1,000 acres) of gardens, walking paths, and woods, as well as three artificial lakes. It's also home to several monuments, including the striking Monumento de los Españoles and one of President Sarmiento (he of the park decree; 1811–1888) by Auguste Rodin (1840–1917). The park is hugely popular with Porteños

Tourists explore the lakes at Parque Tres de Febrero on colorful pedal boats.

of all ages on weekends; some merely sunbathe, stroll, and picnic, while the fitness-minded run, bicycle, and go inline skating. *See bullet* ④, *p. 22.*

⑥ ★★★ **Los Lagos/Rosedal.** Tucked within Parque Tres de Febrero are three manmade lakes, surrounded by eucalyptus trees and *ombú* bushes. You can rent colorful pedal boats and rowboats to get around. Nearby is El Rosedal, a beautiful rose garden designed in 1914 by Thays, with more than 12,000 plantings. Favorite spots include the **Jardín de los Poetas** (Poets' Garden), with small fountains and busts of poets; **Patio Andaluz,** a southern Spain–style tiled terrace; and the ornate **Puente Blanco** (white bridge), a landmark for Porteños. *Av. del Libertador (at Av. Sarmiento).*

⑦ ★★ **Jardín Zoológico.** The city's sprawling but manageable zoo, inaugurated in 1888, is a delight for most families, with large lake areas and indigenous species, including *carpinchos. See bullet* ⑧, *p. 54.*

⑧ ★★ kids **Jardín Botánico Carlos Thays.** The first major work of the French landscape designer now bears his name. Built in 1898, the botanical gardens recently went through some rough years when they felt abandoned, but they are again a lovely spot to duck away from the city traffic to read a book or sip *mate,* as some locals do. The large trees — there are some 5,000 species from around the world — provide welcome relief from the Argentine sun, and you'll also find cacti, orchids, ferns, fountains, classical statues in marble, and a wrought-iron greenhouse. *See bullet* ⑥*, p.23.*

⑨ ★ **Parque Las Heras.** The curious thing about this small park, sandwiched between Palermo high-rises and adorned with palm trees, is that it was once the site of a maximum-security prison. Thankfully for residents, that monstrosity was demolished in the '60s and replaced by something much more neighborly. *Av. Las Heras (at Av. Coronel Diaz).*

⑩ ★ **kids** **Na Serapia.** Pop into this tiny folkloric spot to sample authentic Salteña-style empanadas from northern Argentina, considered the finest in the country. *Av. Las Heras 3357.* ☎ *11/4801-5307. $.*

⑪ ★★ **kids** **Hipódromo de Palermo.** Buenos Aires's grand race track was created in 1876 and can seat 100,000 spectators. Argentina

has long been considered one of the world's finest producers of thoroughbreds, and races (free admission) are held at the track at least twice a week. The biggest date on the race calendar is the annual Gran Premio Nacional in November. *See bullet* ⑪*, p. 38.*

⑫ ★★ **Campo Argentino de Polo.** Since 1893, polo has been played at the Campo Argentino, thought of as the "cathedral of polo." It kicks into high gear during the annual Abierto Argentino de Palermo (Argentine Open) matches held in November. *See bullet* ⑪*, p. 38.*

⑬ **La Rural.** This grand turn-of-the-20th-century stadium is a good place to get a peek at the agricultural soul of Argentina. Originally the parade grounds for the Sociedad Rural Argentina, an association of landowners, it was the site of annual livestock shows and gaucho competitions at a time when Argentina's agriculture created immense wealth. The annual Exposición Agrícola y Ganadera (otherwise known as La Rural, held each July) features gaucho stunts and remains one of the most important agricultural exhibitions in the world. *Av. Las Heras (at Av. Santa Fe).* ☎ *11/4777-5557. www.sra.org.ar. Subte: Plaza Italia (D).*

Admire Argentina's exquisite thoroughbreds at the Hipódromo de Palermo racetrack.

Costanera Sur

1. Fuente de las Nereidas
2. Camino de los Plumerillos
3. Río de la Plata
4. Camino de los Alisos
5. Camino de los Lagartos
6. Carritos de la Costanera Sur

This wetlands preserve at the outer edge of upscale Puerto Madero has a peculiar history. It was formed when sand and other debris from development formed wetlands on the bank of the Río de la Plata. Some 250 resident species of birds followed, and in 1986, the local government declared 350 hectares (865 acres) an Ecological Reserve. However, development pressures continue to threaten it, and several large fires in the reserve have been attributed to those who would like to see the development of Puerto Madero extend farther toward the river. START: **Taxi to Av. Achával Rodríguez (at Migone), Puerto Madero.**

1 ★ Fuente de las Nereidas. This Renaissance-style 1903 sculpture in Carrara marble — by Lola Mora (1866–1936), from Tucumán, in the north of Argentina — was originally slated to grace the Plaza de Mayo, directly in front of the presidential palace and across from the Metropolitan Cathedral, but its nude female figures (representing the birth of Venus) caused an

uproar. Eventually, the sculpture found a permanent home here. *Av. R.V. Peñaloza (at Calabria).*

2 Camino de los Plumerillos. Within the Reserva, there are four walking (and biking) trails of varying length, estimated to take from 45 minutes to 2½ hours on foot (they're 2.2km/1¼ miles to 7.9km/5 miles). This path, to the right of the entry

Practical Matters: Reserva Ecológica Costanera Sur

The Reserva Ecológica is open daily from dawn to dusk, it offers free admission, and you can walk or cycle any of the circuits. Circuit 1 is 2.2km (1¼ miles); Circuit 2, 3.3km (2 miles); Circuit 3, 4.2km (2½ miles); and Circuit 4, 7.9km (5 miles). Free guided tours are offered Saturday and Sunday at 10:30am and 3:30pm. For additional information, call ☎ 11/4893-1588 or visit www.buenosaires. gov.ar. At times, the Reserve feels very isolated and devoid of people, and some locals warn of homeless and occasionally inebriated people who loiter in the Reserve, so it's probably best not to go alone or towards dusk.

gate, forms part of either Circuit 2 (🕐 1 hr.; 3.3km/2 miles) or circuit 4 (🕐 2½ hr.; 7.9km/5 miles). It passes the Laguna de los Patos (Duck Lagoon) and a swamp area that is being restored and incorporated into the Reserva.

3 **Río de la Plata.** The wide and muddy Río de la Plata may not be your idea of a photogenic beach, but plenty of Porteño couples and families venture down to the banks to gaze toward Uruguay.

4 **Camino de los Alisos.** Heading north along the path (and Circuit 4, the long route), you'll pass a *Bosque de Alisos* (alder trees), a marsh area, and red-blossoming *ceibo* trees (the national tree of Argentina).

5 **Camino de los Lagartos.** The final trajectory of Circuit 4, and the second segment of the shortest Circuit 1 (🕐 45 min; 2.2km/1¼ miles), leads past the Laguna de las Gaviotas (Seagull Pond) and back to the Reserva's entrance.

6 **kids** **Carritos de la Costanera Sur.** After that hot and dry walk through the Reserve, the barbecue food carts parked along the Costanera Sur are a welcome sight. They sell soft drinks, water, and beer, but mostly they traffic in *parrillada* (barbecued meats), *choripán* (chorizo sausage on bread), and *bondiola* (pork) sandwiches. *Av. Achával Rodríguez/Boulevard de los Italianos. $.*

Río de la Plata is a popular destination for local families and couples.

Buenos Aires by Bike

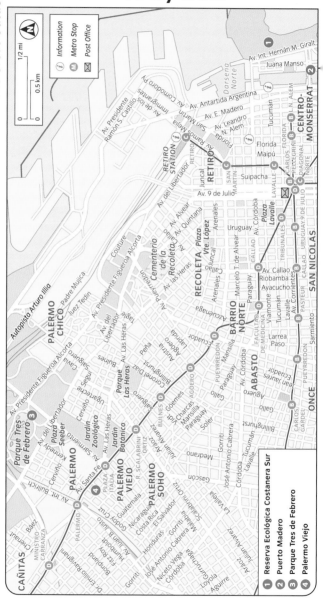

- **1** Reserva Ecológica Costanera Sur
- **2** Puerto Madero
- **3** Parque Tres de Febrero
- **4** Palermo Viejo

Buenos Aires may not be an obviously bike-friendly capital, but it's becoming more so, and several organizations are equipped to rent bicycles and lead two-wheeled tours of the city. Drivers of cars, buses, and taxis aren't yet accustomed to sharing the road, however, so it's best to stick to the following safer areas. The only real bike paths, as of yet, are in the parks.

1 ★★ Reserva Ecológica Costanera Sur. This isolated wetlands preserve of 350 hectares (865 acres), at the outer edge of Puerto Madero, has four dirt walking and biking trails of varying length: 2.2km (1¼ miles); 3.3km (2 miles); 4.2km (2½ miles); and 7.9km (5 miles). The routes pass two lakes known for their birdlife and lead down to the banks of the Río de la Plata, always with a view of Puerto Madero's distant skyscrapers. The reserve is open daily from dawn to dusk. *Av. Costanera Sur (at Av. R.V. Peñaloza).* ☎ *11/4893-1588. www. buenosaires.gov.ar.*

2 ★ Puerto Madero. This fast-growing area of new high-rise residential and commercial towers is still underpopulated. Its wide avenues and new, smooth pavement along the docks, past new restaurants and the Yacht Club, are perfect for cycling with no interference from cars and little from pedestrians. East of the port's docks, you can cycle along the Costanera Sur (Av. Achával Rodríguez and Av. Carlos Noel), at the edge of the Reserva Ecológica, and through a series of three park areas: Parque Micaela Basidas, Parque Vinginia Balten, and Parque de las Mujeres Argentinas. *Av. Alicia Moreau de Justo (at Villaflor).*

3 ★★★ Palermo parks and gardens. Parque Tres de Febrero is the prime destination for cyclists, especially on weekends, when you'll have to contend with inline skaters, runners, baby strollers, horse carriages, and other cyclists. It's a relaxed, wide-open, pretty, and verdant zone. Choose any of the roads that run through the parks, which extend as far as the Hipódromo (race track) and Lago de Regatas (Rowing Lake), or join the multitudes on the circular road (Av. Infanta Isabel, Av. Iraola, and Av. Presidente Mott) around the manmade lakes. *Av del Libertador (at Av. Sarmiento).*

4 ★ Palermo Viejo. This is the one densely populated residential area I'm willing to recommend for cyclists. Though many of the streets are cobblestoned, the barrio has the

The lush Parque Tres de Febrero is the city's top cycling destination.

96

Cycling along the paths of the Reserva Ecológica Costanera Sur wetlands.

kind of laid-back vibe, with fewer cars than other districts, and great shopping and cafe pit stops, that make it perfect for relaxed cycling (more so than exercise cycling). Take a gentle ride through the streets beginning at the Jardín Botánico (see p. 53) and along Jorge Luis Borges to Plaza Julio Cortázar, the main square of Palermo Soho. The railroad tracks mark the boundary of Palermo Hollywood. *Av. Scalabrini Ortiz to Av. Dorrego (between Av. Santa Fe and Av. Cordoba).* ●

Bicycle Rentals & Tours

The following companies rent bikes and lead tours through Buenos Aires:

- **La Bicicleta Naranja** This company really does rent orange bicycles, and it offers themed and guided rides and other circuits (Mon–Fri 9:30am and 2pm; Sat–Sun 2pm), as well as bike rentals. (Pasaje Guiffra, San Telmo & Nicaragua 4825, Palermo. ☎ 11/4362-1104. www.labicicletanaranja.com.ar.)
- **Lan & Kramer Bike Tours** Offers cruiser-style bike rentals and guided circuits, including to Tigre. (Florida 868, 14th floor. ☎ 11/4311-5199. www.biketours.com.ar.)
- **Bicicleterías Saúl** Bike hire and bicyle-tourism outings, with offices near Parque Tres de Febrero. (Boulogne Sur Mer 289 & Libertador 7551, Palermo. ☎ 11/4867-6706.)
- **Urban Biking** Daily tours leaving from Torre de los Ingleses/ Retiro (including a night tour and one to Tigre) and bike rentals. (☎ 11/4568-4321. www.urbanbiking.com.)

Dining Best Bets

Best Steak That Could Feed a Family
★★ La Cabrera $$$ *Cabrera 5099/5127 (p 105)*

Best Museum Restaurant
★★ Café des Arts $$$ *Av. Figueroa Alcorta 3415 (p 102)*; and ★★ Museo Evita Restaurant & Bar $$ *Guitérrez 3926 (p 106)*

Best Seafood
★★★ Crizia $$$ *Gorriti 5143 (p 103)*

Best Empanadas
★★ La Cupertina $ *Cabrera 5300 (p 105)*

Best Working-Class Restaurant with Famous Fans
★★ El Obrero $ *Agustín R. Caffarena 64 (p 104)*

Best (Small) Hotel Restaurant
★★ Bo Bo Restaurant $$ *Guatemala 4882 (p 101)*

Best Fancy French Cuisine
★★★ La Bourgogne $$$$ *Av. Alvear 1891 (p 104)*

Best Argentina's Political Past
★★ El General $$ *Av. Belgrano 561 (p 104)*

Best Retro Stylings
★★ Standard $$ *Guatemala 2003 (p 108)*

Best Steakhouse Splurge
★★ Cabaña Las Lilas $$$$ *Alicia Moreau de Justo 516 (p 102)*

Best Wine List
★★ Casa Cruz $$$ *Uriarte 1658 (p 103)*; and ★★★ La Bourgogne $$$$ *Av. Alvear 1891 (p 104)*

Best Rock 'n Roll Chef
★★★ Café San Juan $$ *Av. San Juan 450 (p 102)*

Best Breakfast
★★ Oui Oui $ *Nicaragua 6099 (p 107)*; and ★★ Bo Bo Restaurant $$ *Guatemala 4882 (p 101)*

Best Unexpected (Nordic) Cuisine
★★ Olsen $$ *Gorriti 5870 (p 107)*

Best Spanish Tapas
★ Tancat $$ *Paraguay 645 (p 108)*; and ★★★ Café San Juan $$ *Av. San Juan 450 (p 102)*

Previous Page: Bo Bo Restaurant is warm, inviting, and has an excellent fixed-price lunch menu.

Tancat is a local favorite, with authentic Spanish tapas.

Centro/San Telmo Dining

Legend:
- (i) Information
- (M) Metro Stop
- ☐ Point of Interest
- ✉ Post Office

Bar El Federal **3**
Brasserie Petanque **5**
Cabaña Las Lilas **9**
Café San Juan **2**
Café Tortoni **7**
El Cuartito **11**
El General **6**
El Obrero **1**
La Americana **8**
La Brigada **4**
Tancat **10**

Recoleta/Palermo Dining

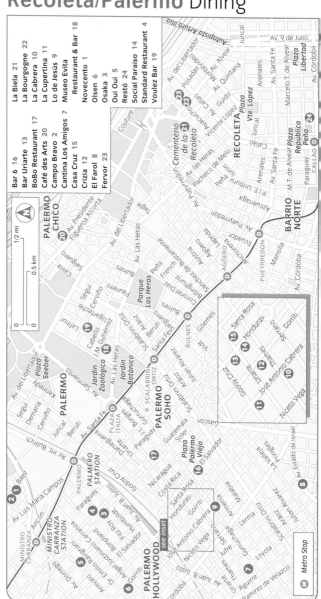

Bar 6 16
Bar Uriarte 13
BoBo Restaurant 17
Café des Arts 20
Campo Bravo 2
Cantina Los Amigos 7
Casa Cruz 15
Crizia 12
El Farol 8
Fervor 23
La Biela 21
La Bourgogne 22
La Cabrera 10
La Cupertina 11
Lo de Jesús 9
Museo Evita
Restaurant & Bar 18
Novecento 1
Olsen 6
Osaka 3
Oui Oui 5
Resto 24
Social Paraíso 14
Standard Restaurant 4
Voulez Bar 19

Buenos Aires **Restaurants A to Z**

★ kids **Bar 6** PALERMO SOHO *INTERNATIONAL* A cool cafe and hipster hangout, perfect for a shopping pit stop, Bar 6 is more ambitious at heart. Breakfast might be a creative fruit shake and croissant, while lunch and dinner center on vegetarian woks, lamb, and grilled salmon. *Armenia 1676.* ☎ *11/4833-6807. Entrees AR$24–AR$50. AE, DC, MC, V. Breakfast, lunch & dinner Mon–Sat. Subte: No access. Map p 100.*

★★ **Bar Uriarte** PALERMO SOHO *MEDITERRANEAN* Enter past the grill and clay oven on the way into this chic, industrial-cool restaurant, considered one of the hippest Palermo eateries. The menu concentrates on homemade pastas, grilled meat, and fish; items from the clay oven are served only at night. *Uriarte 1572.* ☎ *11/4834-6004. Entrees AR$31–AR$43. AE, DC, MC, V. Lunch & dinner daily. Subte: No access. Map p 100.*

★★ **Bo Bo Restaurant** PALERMO SOHO *MEDITERRANEAN* Despite being the restaurant of a seven-room boutique hotel, Bo Bo is as much about eating as it is sleeping. It's a sophisticated and colorful space, with a menu to match: Mediterranean fare with Asian touches and a superb-value fixed-price menu midday. *Guatemala 4882.* ☎ *11/4774-0505. Entrees AR$35–AR$55. AE, DC, MC, V. Breakfast, lunch & dinner daily. Subte: No access. Map p 100.*

★★ kids **Brasserie Petanque** SAN TELMO *FRENCH* This brasserie looks imported from Paris, but it's a handsome recreation: The old-looking patina is new. The classic French menu features steak tartare with frites, rabbit stew, and *boeuf bourguignon*, and there's a children's menu. *Defensa 596 (at México).* ☎ *11/4342-7930. Entrees AR$25–AR$42. AE, DC, MC, V. Lunch Sun–Fri; dinner daily. Subte: Independencia (C). Map p 99.*

Bo Bo's attractive dining room complements the Asian-influenced Mediterranean menu.

Dining Tips

For dinner, Argentines—and particularly Porteños—like Spaniards, eat *very* late. Many fashionable restaurants don't start filling up until 10 or 11pm, even on weekdays. If you sit down to dinner at 8pm, you may find yourself eating virtually alone or joined only by fellow visitors to the city. At nicer restaurants, your bill will include a *cubierto* (also called *servicio de mesa*); essentially, it's the price (anywhere from AR$5–AR$20) to sit down at a table, get your silverware, napkin and bread—but it's definitely not the gratuity, which is extra (usually 10%).

★★ **Cabaña Las Lilas** PUERTO MADERO *ARGENTINE/PARRILLA* Ask Porteños for the best steak in town, and they're likely to point you here. (Even if they say, "Prices are for tourists.") It's famous for the quality of its meat, which comes from the restaurant's private *estancia* (ranch) and is always expertly prepared. *Alicia Moreau de Justo 516 (Dique 3).* ☎ *11/4313-1336. Entrees AR$40–AR$98. AE, V. Lunch & dinner daily. Subte: L.N. Alem (B). Map p 99.*

★★ **Café des Arts** PALERMO *FRENCH* A chic and airy bistro within MALBA (the Museum of Latin American Art), its creative salads and tarts, classic French sandwiches, and more substantial entrees make it a midday destination for plenty of professionals and lunching ladies. *Av. Figueroa Alcorta 3415.* ☎ *11/4808-0754. Entrees AR$28–AR$62. MC, V. Lunch Tues–Sun; dinner daily. Subte: No access. Map p 100.*

★★★ **Café San Juan** SAN TELMO *ARGENTINE/SPANISH* This unpretentious gem seems more homespun than haute cuisine. The extensive menu is delivered to your table on a large chalkboard, a challenge if your Spanish is lacking, but everything—from Spanish tapas to gnocchis and incredible *bondiola de cerdo* (Asian-inflected pork neck)—is outstanding. *Av. San Juan 450.* ☎ *11/4300-1112. Entrees AR$25–AR$40. No credit cards. Lunch & dinner Tues–Sun. Subte: San Juan (C). Map p 99.*

★ **Campo Bravo** LAS CANITAS *ARGENTINE/PARRILLA* An insanely popular spot for good-value steaks served on boards from the wood-fired grill. Though there is a young and fashionable crowd and dance-party soundtrack, it's also great for dependable *parrilla,* salads, and homemade empanadas. *Báez 292 (at Arévalo).* ☎ *11/4514-5820.*

Café San Juan delivers haute cuisine in an unpretentious atmosphere.

Entrees AR$20–AR$38. MC. Lunch Tues–Sun; dinner daily. Subte: Carranza (D). Map p 100.

★ **kids** **Cantina Los Amigos** VILLA CRESPO *ITALIAN* Aptly named, this amiable cantina is where old friends return time and time again for a homey meal of Italian favorites, including raviolis and lemon chicken *(pollo a la Antelo)*. *Loyola 701.* ☎ *11/4777-0422. Entrees AR$18–AR$30. AE, V, M. Lunch Tues–Sun; dinner Mon–Sat. Subte: Malabia (B). Map p 100.*

★★ **Casa Cruz** PALERMO SOHO *INTERNATIONAL* This restaurant looks more like an exclusive nightclub, with its sleek decor and minimalist mood lighting. The food doesn't quite match the design, but the eclectic menu pulls out all the stops, with items like Usuaia King Crab ravioli with pink grapefruit, algae, and coconut cream. The wine list is suitably impressive. *Uriarte 1658 (at Honduras).* ☎ *11/4833-1112. Entrees AR$38–AR$72. AE, MC, V. Dinner daily. Subte: No access. Map p 100.*

★★★ **Crizia** PALERMO SOHO *ARGENTINE/SEAFOOD* A dramatic, soaring space, this is one of the best new restaurants in the city—even though it's not new, merely relocated from a very different locale in the Centro. It's tops for seafood lovers, with an oyster bar and excellent fresh fish, but carnivores will love the grilled meats, such as a superb slow-cooked Patagonian lamb roll. *Gorriti 5143.* ☎ *11/4831-4979. Entrees AR$29–AR$50. AE, MC, V. Lunch Sun; dinner Tues–Sat. Subte: No access. Map p 100.*

★ **kids** **El Cuartito** CENTRO *PIZZA* This is many Porteños' choice for the best traditional pizzas in the city. A simple, loud, and fun place, El Cuartito's been cranking out pizzas since 1934. *Talcahuano 937.* ☎ *11/4816-1758. Entrees AR$18–AR$30. No credit cards. Lunch & dinner daily. Subte: Tribunales (D). Map p 99.*

★ **kids** **El Farol** ALMAGRO *ARGENTINE* An old-school family favorite that isn't fashionable, isn't in a cool neighborhood, and doesn't try to be anything that it's not. It's just a time-tested place where locals go to eat well-prepared, standard Argentine and Italian dishes, such as pastas (raviolis stuffed with vegetables, salmon, and even calves' brains)

El Farol boasts well-prepared, traditional Argentine and Italian dishes.

The Best Dining

and dependable *parrilla*. *Av. Estado de Israel 4488.* ☎ *11/4866-3233. Entrees AR$25–AR$45. AE, DC, MC, V. Lunch Sun; dinner Mon–Sat. Subte: Angel Gallardo (B). Map p 100.*

★★ **El General** MONSERRAT *ARGENTINE* A serious restaurant built around a theme of the legendary General Juan and Evita Perón, the place is loaded with memorabilia about the Argentine first couple that lives on in the memory of many here. It's a surprisingly elegant restaurant (and anything but Peronista working class in its decor!), with white tablecloths, black-tied waiters, excellent *parrilla*, and dishes that El General counted among his favorites. *Av. Belgrano 561 (at Perú).* ☎ *11/4342-7830. Entrees AR$17–AR$90. AE, DC, MC, V. Lunch & dinner Mon–Sat. Subte: Moreno. Map p 99.*

★★ **kids El Obrero** LA BOCA *ITALIAN/PARRILLA* A host of globetrotting celebs, including U2 and the film director Wim Wenders, have dropped in on this deceptively

The homemade meals at El Obrero attract A-list celebrities.

atmospheric spot for great soups, homemade pastas, and well-prepared steaks. The sports paraphernalia littering the walls will remind you that you're only blocks from one of the most famous soccer stadiums in the world, La Bombonera. *Agustin R. Caffarena 64 (at Caboto).* ☎ *11/4362-9912. Entrees AR$10–AR$29. No credit cards. Lunch & dinner Mon–Sat. Subte: No access. Map p 99.*

★ **Fervor** RECOLETA *PARRILLA/ SEAFOOD* A classic-looking, two-level Argentine restaurant that distinguishes itself with its *brasas de campo y mar*—essentially, grilled surf and turf. It's the surf that makes Fervor different from other *parrillas*, and the *parrillada de pescado y mariscos* (grilled seafood and shellfish) is a winner. *Posadas 1519 (at Callao).* ☎ *11/4804-4944. Entrees AR$30–AR$55. AE, DC, M, V. Lunch & dinner daily. Subte: No access. Map p 100.*

kids La Americana CENTRO *ARGENTINE/EMPANADAS* A block from Congress, "La Reina de las Empanadas" (Queen of Empanadas) is where to go for a cheap, fast meal of tasty baked empanadas, an Argentine classic. Pick up your food and drinks separately and stand at a counter—or grab a table at the loud, fast-food-like seating area, where you can also get pizzas and calzones. *Callao 83 (at Bartolomé Mitre).* ☎ *11/4371-0202. Entrees AR $3–AR$23. No credit cards. Breakfast, lunch & dinner daily (until late). Subte: Congreso (A). Map p 99.*

★★★ **La Bourgogne** RECOLETA *CLASSIC FRENCH* Elegant and formal (jacket and tie are required for men), in the city's best-known, high-end hotel, and ridiculously expensive for Buenos Aires: This is the place to go if you want to impress and a destination for discriminating

Dining at a *Café Notable*

More than 50 of Buenos Aires's historic cafes and bars, most dating from the late 19th and early 20th centuries, are designated *cafés notables* and protected by law from being altered or razed. While they're atmospheric places for a coffee or a late-night drink, several also make excellent stops for a full meal. Among the best for breakfast, lunch, or dinner are **Café Tortoni** (Av. de Mayo 825; ☎ 11/4342-4328) the city's oldest cafe; **Bar El Federal** (Carlos Calvo 599; ☎ 11/4300-4313), a San Telmo institution since 1864; and **La Biela** (Av. Quintana 596; ☎ 11/4804-0449), a Parisian-style cafe with a people-watchers' terrace in Recoleta.

gourmands seeking a classic, perfectly executed French meal. Oenophiles should make a point of visiting the superb wine cellar, which holds occasional tastings. *Av. Alvear 1891 (Alvear Palace Hotel). ☎ 11/4805-3857. www.alvear palace.com. Main courses AR$80–AR$98. AE, DC, MC, V. Lunch Mon–Fri; dinner Mon–Sat. Closed Jan. Subte: No access. Map p 100.*

★ **La Brigada** SAN TELMO *PARRILLA* A longtime favorite among visitors to San Telmo, this *parrilla* goes whole hog on the Argentine pampas myth, with tango music and gaucho memorabilia. Though the *lomo* (sirloin steak) and baby beef don't disappoint, some diners may find the restaurant touristy. *Estados Unidos 465 (at Bolívar). ☎ 11/4361-5557. Entrees AR$22–AR$40. AE, DC, MC, V. Lunch & dinner daily. Subte: Constitución (C). Map p 99.*

★★ **La Cabrera** PALMERO SOHO *ARGENTINE/PARRILLA* Buenos Aires is littered with *parrillas,* but none is as consistently popular as this one, which packs diners into two locations just steps apart. (They take reservations only until 9pm; after that, it's a certain long wait.) Exquisitely cooked meat is served in enormous portions on wooden

slabs, along with a distinctive array of condiments: spreads, sauces, and olives, among other items. *Cabrera 5099 & 5127 (at Thames). ☎ 11/4831-7002. Entrees AR $25–AR$40. AE, DC, MC, V. Lunch & dinner Tues–Sun. Subte: No access. Map p 100.*

★ **kids La Cupertina** PALERMO SOHO *NORTHERN ARGENTINE/EMPANADAS* This is my favorite spot in the capital to sample the distinctive variety of empanadas from

La Cupertina serves distinctive empanadas at a slow and steady pace.

The enticing Lo de Jesús parilla.

Tucumán, a northern province; they're juicy and spicy, and impossible to stop eating at around a dollar apiece. The adorable cafe, with its charismatic owner, goes about its business at its own pace, frustrating many—but it's well worth the wait. *Cabrera 5300 (at Godoy Cruz).* ☎ *11/4777-3711. Entrees AR$12–AR15. No credit cards. Lunch & dinner Tues–Sat; lunch only (winter) Sun; dinner only (summer) Sun. Subte: No access. See map p 100.*

★★ **Lo de Jesús** PALERMO SOHO *PARILLA* A seductive-looking place, inhabiting a 1953 Palermo grocer, with a black-and-white checkered floor, large old mirrors, and chalkboards with menu items written in pastel swirls. Though primarily a *parrilla,* non-meat eaters won't be disappointed with the excellent *pacú,* a large river fish. *Gurruchaga 1406 (at Cabrera).* ☎ *11/4831-1961. Entrees AR$25–AR$40. AE, V, MC. Lunch & dinner daily. Subte: No access. Map p 100.*

★★ kids **Museo Evita Restaurant & Bar** PALERMO *ARGENTINE BISTRO* A delightful, casual little bistro attached to Museo Evita. Many, if not most, of its diners are locals who aren't visiting the

museum—just coming for the lovely and verdant outdoor terrace (beautifully illuminated at night) and the simple but well-prepared and inexpensive fare, which includes gorgeous salads, homemade pastas, and a few steak and grilled fish options. *J.M. Guitérrez 3926.* ☎ *11/ 4800-1599. Entrees AR$15–AR$35. AE, V, MC. Breakfast, lunch & dinner daily. Subte: Plaza Italia (D). Map p 100.*

★ **Novecento** LAS CANITAS *INTERNATIONAL* A curiosity, this romantic, affordable New York–style bistro restaurant is a pioneer in the happening Las Cañitas district, and an undeniable hit among the fashionable elite in Buenos Aires. There are recognizably Argentine items on the menu, such as empanadas, but also international dishes popular across the globe, including risottos, stuffed cannelloni, paella, and grilled Pacific salmon. *Báez 199 (at Arguibel).* ☎ *11/4778-1900. Entrees AR$20–AR$34. AE, DC, MC, V. Lunch & dinner daily; brunch Sun. Subte: Carranza (D). Map p 100.*

The fashionable Novecento bistro serves Argentine and International cuisine.

The menu at Social Paraiso restaurant is limited but excellent.

★★ Olsen PALERMO VIEJO *SCAN-DINAVIAN/SEAFOOD*   This hipster destination is a soaring old warehouse set back from the street, with a minimalist, mid-century modern design. For those tired of the too-common *parrillada*-and-red-wine routine, Olsen is a good antidote, with excellent salmon tartare, tuna steaks, smoked herring, and a long list of specialty vodkas. The Sunday brunch is hugely popular with recovering clubbers. *Gorriti 5870 (at Carranza).* ☎ *11/4776-7677. Entrees AR$27–AR$58. AE, DC, MC, V. Lunch Tues–Sat; dinner Tues–Sun; brunch Sun. Subte: No access. Map p 100.*

★★ Osaka PALERMO HOLLYWOOD *PERUVIAN/JAPANESE*   Originating in Lima, Peru—where Japanese fusion has long informed the best Peruvian cooking—this smart two-story restaurant with an outdoor terrace upstairs is the best place in town for sushi and ceviche. Not a fan of raw fish? No problem, there are plenty of Asian fusion dishes with an exotic twist, such as stuffed squid, woks, and grilled seafood. *Soler 5608 (at Fitz Roy).* ☎ *11/4775-6964. Entrees AR$30–AR$45. MC, V. Lunch & dinner Mon–Sat. Subte: No access. Map p 100.*

★★ kids Oui Oui PALERMO HOLLYWOOD *FRENCH BISTRO*   An adorable set of twin cafes on the same street, these easygoing spots are perfect for a relaxing lunch of great French sandwiches, salads, vegetarian options, fresh-baked goods, and excellent coffee and juices. *Nicaragua 6099 (at Dorrego).* ☎ *11/4778-9614. Entrees AR$15–AR$28. No credit cards. Breakfast, lunch & early dinner Tues–Fri; brunch, lunch & dinner Sat–Sun. Subte: No access. Map p 100.*

★★★ Restó BARRIO NORTE *HAUTE ARGENTINE*   Despite a hidden location, very odd hours, and a cash-only policy, this tiny, elegant cafe ensconced within the Argentine Society of Architects is one of the finest restaurants in Buenos Aires. Featuring a small but creative daily menu and just a dozen tables, it's a favorite of local architects and some of the city's most discriminating palates. Mostly a lunch affair, it's open just two nights a week. *Montevideo 938.* ☎ *11/4816-6711. Entrees AR$28–AR$78. No credit cards. Lunch Mon–Fri; dinner Thur & Fri. Subte: Callao (D). Map p 100.*

★★ Social Paraiso PALERMO SOHO *ARGENTINE*   Intriguingly plain and intimate, this tiny restaurant has

The charming twin Oui Oui cafes are great for coffee or lunch.

large windows and an intense focus on a limited but excellent menu that changes daily. The emphasis is on grilled meat but always includes fresh fish and inventive vegetarian entrees, often with Middle-Eastern influences—a refreshing change from the imposing scenester places that abound these days in Palermo Viejo. *Honduras 5182.* ☎ 11/4831-4556. *Entrees AR$25–AR$40. MC, V. Lunch Tues–Sun; dinner Tues–Sat. Subte: No access. Map p 100.*

★★ **Standard Restaurant** PAL-ERMO HOLLYWOOD *ARGENTINE* The look of this terrific restaurant—retro-modern and minimalist mid-century dining hall—may be too stark for some. The dishes, too (like the beet salad, breaded veal, and raviolis stuffed with calves' brains), have a retro sensibility—you half feel as though you should be wearing a grey flannel suit and a fedora—but they're very well done. *Guatemala 2003 (at Fitz Roy).* ☎ 11/4779-2774. *Entrees AR$26–AR$48. AE, MC, V. Dinner Mon–Sat; lunch Sat. Subte: No access. Map p 100.*

★ **Tancat** CENTRO *SPANISH/ TAPAS* A few blocks from Calle Florida's retail overload, this Spanish *tasca* restaurant may not sound welcoming (the name means "closed" in Catalan), but it's generally bustling, packed with midday and late-night diners sampling a long list of authentic Spanish tapas and a great menu of daily specials, like suckling pig and grilled squid. *Paraguay 645.* ☎ 11/4312-5442. *Entrees AR$15–AR$50. AE, MC, V. Lunch & dinner daily. Subte: San Martín (C). Map p 99.*

★ **Voulez Bar** PALERMO *ARGEN-TINE* Voulez Bar (a play on "boulevard" in Spanish) is effortlessly chic, and it seems like everyone here is a regular who comes for a small menu of what they know is a well-prepared and reasonably priced meal of Asian-inflected entrees, fresh salads, and tasty sandwiches. A nice, sunny place to linger over morning coffee and light breakfast, too. *Boulevard Cerviño 3802.* ☎ 11/4802-4817. *Entrees AR$22–AR$45. AE, MC, V. Breakfast, lunch & dinner daily. Subte: Plaza Italia (D). Map p 100.* ●

Tancat is a favorite spot for late-night dining.

Nightlife Best Bets

Best Place for Watering-Hole Graffiti
★★ Bar Plaza Dorrego, *Defensa 1096* (p 113)

Best Old-School Tango Dance Hall
★★★ El Niño Bien, *Humberto I no. 1462* (p 118); and ★★ Sunderland Club, *Lugones 3161* (p 118)

Best Decadent Cocktail Lounge
★★ Club 647, *Tacuarí 647* (p 114)

Best Dance-Club Soundtrack
★★ Niceto Club, *Niceto Vega 5510* (p 116)

Best Hotel Bar (Large & Small)
★★ Bar del Hotel Alvear, *Av. Alvear 1891* (p 113); and ★★ Home Hotel, *Honduras 5860* (p 114)

Some of the best cocktails in town can be found at San Telmo's Club 647.

Best Employment of a Mississippi Riverboat
★ Casino Flotante, *Elvira Rawson de Dellepina, Dársena Sur* (p 115)

Best Gay Restaurant-Bar
★ Chueca, *Soler 3283* (p 117)

Best Place for A Creative Cocktail List and Bartenders
★★ Gran Bar Danzón, *Libertad 1161* (p 114); and ★★★ Club 647, *Tacuarí 647* (p 114)

Best Irish Pub
★★ Shamrock, *Rodríguez Peña 1220* (p 115)

Best Funky Cocktail Bar Named After a Hollywood Legend
★★ Kim y Novak, *Güemes 4900* (p 114)

Best Late-Night Pool Hall
★★ 36 Billares, *Av. de Mayo 1265* (p 113)

Best Bar You Might Want to Live In
★★ Milión, *Paraná 1048* (p 115)

Best Outdoor Tango Scene
★★★ La Glorieta, *11 de Septiembre* (p 118)

Best Gay Club for You and 1,000 New Friends
★★ Amerika, *Gascón 1040* (p 116)

Best Tango Salon Fit for a Movie Set
★★ Confitería Ideal, *Suipacha 384* (p 117)

Previous page: Dressing to impress for a night of tango.

Centro/San Telmo Nightlife

Alsina 10
Asia de Cuba 12
Bar El Federal 4
Bar Plaza Dorrego 3
Bar Seddón 6
Casino Flotante 2
Club 647 8
Confiteria Ideal 13
Cosmo Bar by Axel 7
El Niño Bien 9
La Perla 1
Le Bar 14
Tango Queer 5
The Kilkenny 15
36 Billares 11

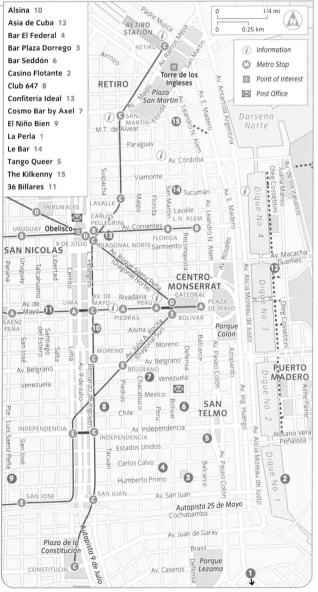

0   1/4 mi
0   0.25 km

(i) Information
(M) Metro Stop
▢ Point of Interest
✉ Post Office

Palermo Nightlife

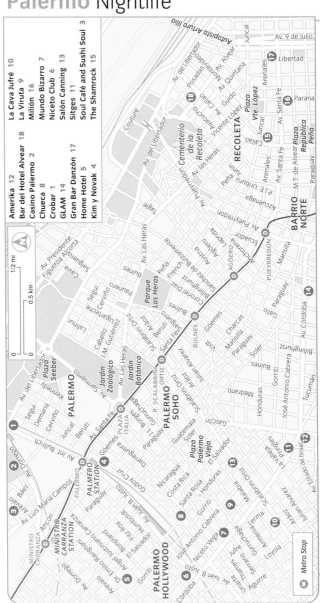

Buenos Aires Nightlife A to Z

Historic Cafe-Bars

★★★ Bar El Federal SAN TELMO The epitome of cool, this cafe, circa 1864 (and protected by law as a *café notable*), has a fantastically elaborate carved-wood bar and antique cash registers; good food and a great place to wile away the afternoon or night. *Carlos Calvo 599.* ☎ *11/4300-4313. Subte: Independencia (C). Map p 111.*

★★ Bar del Hotel Alvear RECOLETA A sumptuous lobby bar at the city's most traditional and prestigious hotel, the room is rich in chandeliers, thick drapes, and sophisticated drinks. *Av. Alvear 1891.* ☎ *11/4808-2100. Subte: No access. Map p 112.*

★★ Bar Plaza Dorrego SAN TELMO A time-honored, nostalgic watering hole that's scruffy and cool, with generations of graffiti scratched onto the walls. It's a zoo on Sundays during the Antiques Fair, but laid-back the rest of the week. *Defensa 1096.* ☎ *11/4361-0141. Subte: Independencia (C). Map p 111.*

★★ Bar Seddón SAN TELMO Once a pharmacy back in the 19th century, this atmospheric cafe-bar has live blues, jazz, and tango performances at night. In the early evening, it's a calm spot to read or write postcards, but it gets quite a

The historic Bar del Hotel Alvear is inside the city's most prestigious hotel.

bit more lively as the evening wears on. *Defensa 695, San Telmo.* ☎ *11/4342-3700. Subte: Independencia (C). Map p 111.*

★★ La Perla LA BOCA A 1920s cantina plastered with old photographs, mirrors, and artwork, and colorful seltzer bottles on the tables. Great spot for a rather pricey beer and windows onto touristy La Boca. *Av. Pedro de Mendoza 1899.* ☎ *11/4301-2985. Subte: No access. Map p 111.*

★★ 36 Billares MONSERRAT Billiards live on downstairs in this 1894

Patrons enjoy a game at 36 Billares.

Club 647's striking backlit bar.

institution. It's very old-school, but a great place to drink in some timeless Buenos Aires ambience upstairs. *Av. de Mayo 1265.* ☎ *11/4381-5696. Subte: Saenz Peña (A). Map p 111.*

Bars, Pubs & Lounges

★★★ **Club 647** SAN TELMO   A chi-chi dinner club, this designer's vision of Shanghai in the '30s is also a swank lounge, with deep booths, sexy photos, a red backlit bar, and smashing cocktails. *Tacuarí 647.* ☎ *11/4331-2950. Subte: Belgrano (E). Map p 111.*

★★★ **Gran Bar Danzón** BARRIO NORTE   This fashionable upstairs bar/restaurant, by the backers of the sleek restaurants Sucre and Bar Uriarte, is dark, chic, and has great cocktails, as well as one of the city's best wine lists. *Libertad 1161.* ☎ *11/4811-1108. Subte: Callao (D). Map p 112.*

★★ **Home Hotel** PALERMO SOHO   This boutique hotel also operates a cool little open-air bar overlooking the pool out back. With good snacks, great music (one of the owners is a DJ), and a hip crowd, it's a great early-evening spot (it closes down by midnight for the privacy of guests). *Honduras 5860.* ☎ *11/4778-1008. Subte: No access. Map p 112.*

The Kilkenny RETIRO   A long-time favorite among the city's Irish pubs, with a good mix of locals and foreigners, and of course, Guinness, Kilkenny, and Harp on tap. Live bands every night late. *Marcelo T. de Alvear 399.* ☎ *11/4312-9179. Subte: San Martín (C). Map p 111.*

★★ **Kim y Novak** PALERMO SOHO   A funky and fun place for an entertaining evening, this lounge bar, popular with a gay crowd and alternative types, always has something wild going on to complement its good tunes and even better drinks. *Güemes 4900.* ☎ *11/4773-7521. Subte: No access. Map p 112.*

★ **La Cava Jufré** VILLA CRESPO   For a city and country so identified with local wine, it's odd that Buenos Aires isn't overflowing with wine bars. This is a start to rectifying that, with a nice bottle selection, tavern feel, and outdoor tables. *Jufré 201.* ☎ *11/4775-7501. Subte: Dorrego (B). Map p 112.*

The stylish Milión bar and restaurant.

★★ Le Bar CENTRO A sleek cocktail bar owned by the folks behind the Scandinavian restaurant Olsen, this cool space with great art, in a colonial-style building, has a rooftop terrace with beanbag chairs and fashionable DJs. Great food, too. *Tucumán 422.* ☎ *11/5219-0858. Subte: Florida (B). Map p 111.*

★★ Milión BARRIO NORTE A handsomely converted and sleekly lit old town house, this swank bar and restaurant (with a garden patio) oozes with style and still attracts the beautiful people a decade after its opening. *Paraná 1048.* ☎ *11/4815-9925. Subte: Callao (D). Map p 112.*

★ Mundo Bizarro PALERMO SOHO The name may promise something other-worldly, but this artsy, red-lighted lounge bar is simply one of the city's coolest places for a creative concoction from the extensive cocktail list. Best mid-week. *Serrano 1222.* ☎ *11/4773-1967. Subte: No access. Map p 112.*

★★ The Shamrock RECOLETA Despite the name, this Irish bar will have you thinking you're at a stylish Dublin bar, rather than wading through Guinness at a cheesy theme-park pub. The downstairs Basement Club draws a chic crowd. *Rodríguez Peña 1220.* ☎ *11/4812-3584. Subte: No access. Map p 112.*

★ Soul Café and Sushi Soul LAS CAÑITAS A fashionable young crowd hits this funk-and-soul bar in the heart of the Las Cañitas restaurant and bar scene. There's a bar and a lounge zone, often with live music. *Báez 352.* ☎ *11/4776-3905. Subte: Carranza (D). Map p 112.*

Casinos

Casino Flotante PUERTO MADERO Officially called Casino Puerto Madero, but referred to by most as the "Floating Casino," this huge 24-hour casino inhabits a

La Cava Jufré wine bar offers an excellent selection of fine local wines.

triple-decker old Mississippi riverboat off-shore, east of the docks of Puerto Madero. The casino has more than 100 gaming tables and 700 slot machines. *Elvira Rawson de Dellepina, Dársena Sur.* ☎ *11/4363-3100. Subte: No access. Map p 111.*

Casino Palermo PALERMO Onsite at the Hipódromo Argentino de Palermo (horse race track), this elegant casino has 750 slot machines and a restaurant, and is open 24 hours. And, of course, you can always bet on the horses. *Av. Libertador 4101.* ☎ *11/4778-2800. www.palermo.com.ar. Subte: No access. Map p 112.*

Dance/Nightclubs (Boliches)

Asia de Cuba PUERTO MADERO Business execs and tourists decamped in upscale Puerto Madero populate the dance floor of this restaurant that evolves into a nightclub as the night wears on, playing old-school hits and Latin house music. *Pierina Dealessi 750 (Dique 3).* ☎ *11/4671-9310. www. asiadecuba.com.ar. Subte: No access. Map p 111.*

The scene at the popular Crobar disco, a massive and elaborate club in Palermo.

★ **Crobar** PALERMO   A massive disco with sister clubs in North America, this place is a world unto itself, with upscale devotees who swarm to the VIP lounges, overhead balconies, and walkways. Quite the scene on Friday nights. *Paseo de la Infanta (Av. Libertador 3883).* ☎ *11/4778-1500. www.crobar.com. Fri & Sat. Subte: No access. Map p 112.*

★★ **Niceto Club** PALERMO HOLLYWOOD   Musically speaking, this is one of the hippest dance clubs in Buenos Aires. With two rooms (Side A and Side B) pumping out an eclectic mix of sounds (including live music), there's something for every trendy hipster, from hip-hop to indie rock, and a happening dance floor. *Niceto Vega 5510.* ☎ *11/4779-9396. www.nicetoclub.com. Thurs–Sat. Subte: No access. Map p 112.*

★★ **Pachá** COSTANERA NORTE This massive club along the Río de la Plata, on the outskirts of Buenos Aires, is one of the original denizens of the city's surging nightlife scene, and incredibly, it's still going strong. It's related to the famously hedonistic location in Ibiza, and the party people might not be able to tell the difference. *Av. Costanera Rafael Obligado y La Pampa, Costanera Norte.* ☎ *11/4788-4280. www. pachabuenosaires.com. Subte: No access.*

Gay & Lesbian Bars/Clubs

★ **Alsina** MONSERRAT   A long-time gay favorite, after two name changes (most recently Palacio), it's still in the same impressive space, a large erstwhile factory, with a pretty hot dance scene. *Alsina 934.* ☎ *11/4331-3231. Fri–Sun. Subte: Av. de Mayo (A). Map p 111.*

★★ **Amerika** VILLA CRESPO   Buenos Aires's largest and most popular gay dance club, with a hedonistic playground/party vibe and many hundreds of souls of every possible persuasion on the prowl. *Gascón 1040.* ☎ *11/4865-4416. Fri–Sun. Subte: Angel Gallardo (B). Map p 112.*

★ **Cosmo Bar by Axel** SAN TELMO   One of the axes of the new gay scene in San Telmo is the "hetero-friendly" Axel Hotel. The swank boutique hotel has a chill-out lounge that's popular not just with guests, but with locals and other visitors, as well. The Sky Bar by the pool holds a Sunday-evening pool party. *Venezuela 649.* ☎ *11/4136-9383. Subte: Belgrano (E). Map p 111.*

Milonga Practical Information

Milongas are tango nights at traditional salons or dancehalls; there are more than 150 operating in the city, and most traditional *milongas* have a cover charge from AR$5 to AR$20. Many offer dance classes for novices early in the evening. Once the regulars shuffle in, selecting a partner is all about eye contact, as there's often very little in the way of verbal exchange. For more information about the scene, tangophiles should visit www.todotango. com, www.tangobuenosaires.gob.ar, www.abctango.com.ar, www. tangoqueer.com (for same-sex couple *milongas*), and www.tango focus.com (for tango tours). Several widely available free magazines publish tango info (including instructors, weekly schedules, and classes): *El Tangauta* (www.eltangauta.com), *Diostango* (www. diostango.com.ar), and *B.A. Tango.*

Tango lessons: Offered at many *milongas* and by many teachers in BA, including **Mora Godoy Tango Escuela** (Av. Pueyrredón 1090, Piso 2°A, Recoleta; ☎ 11/4964-0254; www.moragodoy.com) and **Tanguería El Beso** (Riobamba 416, Piso 1°, Once; ☎ 11/4953-2794), run by Susana Miller, who also teaches in the U.S.

Tango attire: Including shoes. See "Tango Specialty Shops" on p 85.

★★ **Chueca** PALERMO SOHO A gay resto-bar (combo bar and restaurant) named after Madrid's hip and largely gay barrio, this chic restaurant serves great Mediterranean fare and *parillada,* and becomes a hopping bar after midnight. Also, check out Chueca's downtown, and Puerto Madero's bars and yacht club. *Honduras 5255.* ☎ *11/4834-6373. Subte: No access. Map p 112.*

★★ **GLAM** BARRIO NORTE A very popular (i.e. crowded) dance club with a wide-ranging clientele, including lots of foreign residents and visitors to the city, although few women and drag queens. The dance floor doesn't get cranking until the wee hours. *Cabrera 3046.* ☎ *11/4963-2521. Subte: Aguero (D). Map p 112.*

Sitges BARRIO NORTE This gay bar features comedy drag shows and unlimited cheap booze for only AR$20. A place to wet your whistle before moving on to one of the big dance clubs. *Av. Cordoba 4119.* ☎ *11/4861-3763. Subte: Angel Gallardo (B).*

Milongas (Tango Dancehalls)

★ **Club Gricel** SAN CRISTÓBAL A traditional, serious *milonga* dancehall—about 3km west of San Telmo—with lots of regulars looking for partners during the week and popular with couples on weekends. *La Rioja 1180.* ☎ *11/4957-7157. Mon–Wed & Sat–Sun from 9pm; Thurs from 7pm. Subte: No access.*

★★ **Confiteria Ideal** CENTRO An antique pastry and coffee shop full of Vienna-style mirrors and Havana-style beautiful dilapidation, this famous place (having made appearances in nearly every

The city's boasts over 150 milongas for every kind of tango lover.

big-budget flick set in Buenos Aires) has almost entirely given itself over to the tango craze. There are classes and *milongas* almost every hour of the day after a few brief morning hours as a cafe. Attracts more tourists than others, but it's a must-do experience. *Suipacha 384.* ☎ *11/5265-8069. www.confiteria ideal.com. Subte: Diagonal Norte (C). Map p 111.*

★★★ **El Niño Bien** CONSTI- TUCIÓN/SAN TELMO   El Niño Bien is one of the most cinematic tango halls in the capital, a gorgeously worn Belle Epoque space with golden walls, mirrors and high ceilings, and a large dance floor surrounded by crowded tables. Thursday's the big circuit night here, after 11pm. *Humberto I no. 1462 (Centro Región Leonesa).* ☎ *11/4483-2588. Subte: No access. Map p 111.*

★★★ **La Glorieta** BELGRANO An unlikely member of the tango

circuit, this open-air gazebo in a park (Barrancas de Belgrano, 3 km. northwest of the Hipódromo) is a glorious change of pace. Classes begin around 6pm on Saturdays and Sundays, and then as dusk falls, the regulars, including a noticeable con- tingent of tango-fanatic foreigners, begin to roll in. A great time, and perhaps best for those who just want to watch. *11 de Septiembre (between Sucre & Echeverria).* ☎ *11/4674-1026. Subte: No access.*

★★ **La Viruta** PALERMO SOHO Dancing tango in the basement of the Armenian Community Center may not sound too sexy, but this all- ages *milonga* is a local favorite, with occasional salsa and other dance detours. Wednesday and Friday nights are big with regulars. *Arme- nia 1366.* ☎ *11/4774-6357. www. lavirutatango.com. Subte: No access. Map p 112.*

★★ **Salón Canning** PALERMO SOHO   One of the most authentic *milongas* in Buenos Aires, this large hall has a great parquet dance floor and legions of fans who take tango very seriously. The Saturday-night "Parakultural" *milonga* is hugely popular. *Scalabrini Ortiz 1331, at Gorriti.* ☎ *11/4832-6753. www. parakultural.com.ar. Mon, Tues & Fri from 10pm; Thur, Sat & Sun from 9pm. Subte: No access. Map p 112.*

★★ **Sunderland Club** VILLA URQUIZA   Reputed to be that tango fanatic Robert Duval's favorite *milonga* in the city (the actor's wife is an Argentine dancer), this utterly traditional dancehall is a hike (8 km northwest of Palermo Soho), but it's where committed practitioners of tango arts can be found Saturday nights. *Lugones 3161.* ☎ *11/4541- 9776. www.sunderlandclub.com.ar. Subte: No access.* ●

Arts & Entertainment Best Bets

Best **Ballet with an Argentine Accent**
★★★ Julio Bocca Ballet Argentino, *Esmeralda 449 (p 125)*

Best **Jaw-Dropping Opera House**
★★★ Teatro Colón, *Libertad 621 (p 124)*

Best **Historic Cafe with Bonus Tango**
★★★ Café Tortoni, *Av. de Mayo 825 (p 129)*

Best **Alternative Music Venue with a Latin Twist**
★★ La Trastienda, *Balcarce 460 (p 127)*

Best **Fútbol Extravaganza**
★★★ El Superclásico, *Brandsen 805 (La Bombonera)/Av. Figueroa Alcorta 7597 (Estadio Monumental) (p 128)*

The city's oldest coffee shop, Café Tortoni, has nightly tango shows.

Best **Quintessential Argentine Horse Spectacle**
★★ Abierto de Polo, *Av. del Libertador (at Av. Dorrego) (p 127)*

Best **Venue for Pro Tango Moves**
★★★ Esquina Carlos Gardel, *Carlos Gardel 3200 (p 130)*

Best **Intimate Jazz Club**
★★ Thelonious Club, *Salguero 1884 (p 127)*

Best **History of Tango Show**
★ El Querandí, *Perú 302 (p 129)*

Best **Movie House for Film Buffs**
★★ Cosmos, *Av. Corrientes 2046 (p 126)*

Best **Shopping Center Culture**
★★ Centro Cultural Borges, *Galerías Pacífico (Viamonte at San Martín) (p 124)*

Best **Belle-Epoque Tango Palace**
★★ Piazzolla Tango, *Florida 165 (p 130)*

Previous Page: Esquina Carlos Gardel is one of the flashiest tanguerías in Buenos Aires, with a good orchestra.

Palermo Arts & Entertainment

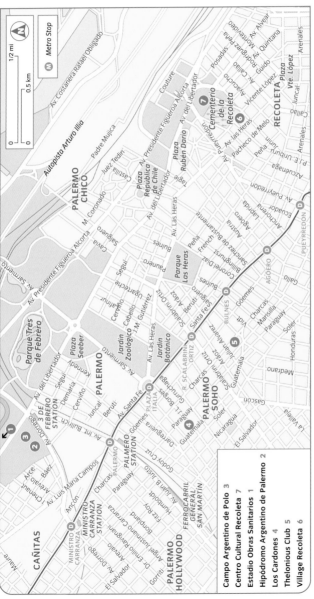

Campo Argentino de Polo 3
Centro Cultural Recoleta 7
Estadio Obras Sanitarios 1
Hipódromo Argentino de Palermo 2
Los Cardones 4
Thelonious Club 5
Village Recoleta 6

122

Centro Arts & Entertainment

The Best Arts & Entertainment

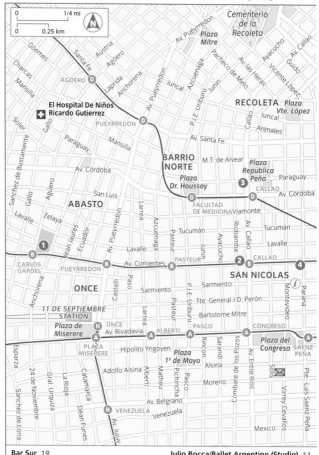

Bar Sur 19

Café La Puerto Rico 15

Café Tortoni 8

Centro Cultural Borges 12

Clásica y Moderna 3

Club Atlético Boca Juniors 20

Cosmos 2

El Querandí 16

El Viejo Almacén 18

Esquina Carlos Gardel 1

Julio Bocca/Ballet Argentino (Theatre) 10

Julio Bocca/Ballet Argentino (Studio) 11

La Trastienda 17

Luna Park 14

Piazzolla Tango 13

Señor Tango 21

Teatro Avenida 7

Teatro Colón 6

Teatro Ópera 9

Teatro Nacional Cervantes 5

Teatro San Martin 4

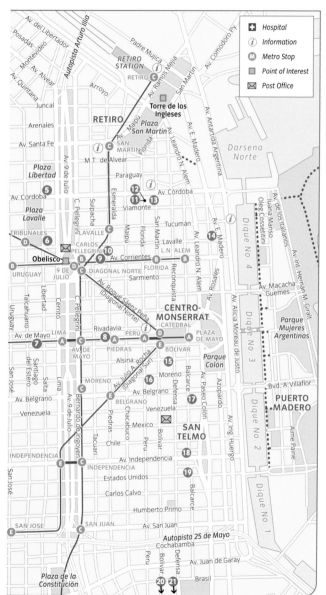

Buenos Aires Arts & Entertainment A to Z

Classical Music & Opera

★★ Teatro Avenida MONSER-RAT   This historic theater, reopened after a devastating fire, is home to Buenos Aires Lírica (the city opera), and it hosts a wide array of cultural performances, including theater, orchestral music, and dance. *Av. de Mayo 1222.* ☎ *11/4812-6369. Tickets AR$6–AR$35. Subte: Saenz Peña (A). Map p 122.*

★★★ Teatro Colón CENTRO A stunning opera house, which recently celebrated its 100th anniversary (and just reopened after a major, lengthy renovation), this has been the stage for operatic greats like Pavarotti, Callas, Domingo, and many more, as well as greats of ballet and classical music. The season is generally from April to November.

Teatro Avenida hosts the opera company and other cultural performances.

Check the website for information and scheduled events, including tours. *Libertad 621.* ☎ *11/4378-7100. www.teatrocolon.org.ar. Tickets AR$15–AR$95. Subte: Tribunales (D). Map p 122.*

★ Teatro Opera CENTRO   The stage of this theater, which opened in 1872, has welcomed everyone from Ella Fitzgerald to tango legends, as well as pop performers and Broadway-style productions. *Av. Corrientes 860.* ☎ *11/4326-1335. Tickets AR$12–AR$65. Subte: Carlos Pellegrini (B). Map p 122.*

Cultural Center Performances

★★ Centro Cultural Borges CENTRO   Amid the glitzy retail shops of Galerías Pacífico is an unexpected arts center named for Argentina's literary giant, with art galleries, an art-house movie theater, and the Julio Bocca Ballet Argentino studio. There are numerous art exhibitions and performances, including tango and flamenco. *Galerías Pacífico (Viamonte at San Martín).* ☎ *11/5555-5359. www.ccborges.org.ar. Admission: AR$10; students and seniors, AR$7. Subte: Florida (B) or San Martín (C). Map p 122.*

★★ Centro Cultural Recoleta RECOLETA   A vibrant cultural center hosting a wide range of art exhibitions, theater, and music concerts —including some cutting-edge stuff, everything from a mix of tango and circus to electronic music and clowns performing contemporary dance. *Junín 1930.* ☎ *11/4803-1041. http://centroculturalrecoleta.org. Free admission. Subte: No access. Map p 121.*

here and a theater performance space with a range of cultural performances. Bocca, an international superstar, is only rarely in Buenos Aires, but the Ballet Argentino troupe is outstanding, and Bocca Tango incorporates traditional tango music and dance. *Studio Julio Bocca: Centro Cultural Borges, Galerías Pacífico, Viamonte at San Martín;* ☎ *11/4315-7558; subte: Florida (B) or San Martin (C). Theater: Teatro Maipo, Esmeralda 449;* ☎ *11/4394-5521; subte: Lavalle (C). Tickets AR$20–AR$105. www.julio bocca.com. Map p 122.*

★★ Teatro Nacional Cervantes CENTRO

A stunning, 80-year-old theater—worth a visit for the building itself—hosting excellent dramatic and dance productions, including *La Señora Macbeth* and *Ciao Tango!*, as well as occasional film cycles. *Av. Córdoba 1155.* ☎ *11/4816-4224. Tickets AR$15–AR$65. www.teatrocervantes.gov.ar. Subte: Tribunales (D). Map p122.*

The 1872 Teatro Opera has welcomed everyone from Ella Fitzgerald to tango legends.

Dance & Theater

★★★ Julio Bocca/Ballet Argentino CENTRO

One of the world's greatest ballet stars, Julio Bocca, operates a studio for classical dance

Theater and dance productions are held at the stunning Teatro Nacional Cervantesis.

Teatro San Martín offers everything from kids' theater to contemporary ballet.

★ Teatro San Martín CENTRO
A soup-to-nuts entertainment complex with three theaters and drama, comedy, dance, music, theater, and art film programs. It has its own contemporary ballet company, theater designed for kids, and occasionally avant-garde music programs, such as concerts of John Cage's minimalist music. *Av. Corrientes 1530.* ☎ *0800/333-5254. Tickets AR$15–AR$50. www.teatrosanmartin.com.ar. Subte: Uruguay (B). Map p 122.*

Film
★★ Cosmos BARRIO NORTE A
landmark movie theater along Av. Corrientes, which was once awash in grand old cinemas. Today, it calls itself a "cultural space" and is much prized by film fans who come to see both classic and art films, as well as new Argentine movies. *Av. Corrientes 2046.* ☎ *11/4953-5405. Tickets AR$11–AR$15. www.cinecosmos.com.ar. Subte: Callao (B). Map p 122.*

Village Recoleta RECOLETA A large multiplex with 16 screens projecting new American, European, and Latin American releases; and a repertoire of bars and restaurants, and a bookstore. *Vicente López 2050.* ☎ *810/810-2463. Tickets AR$15–AR$20. www.villagecines.com. Subte: No access. Map p 121.*

Live Music (Jazz/Rock/Pop)
★ Clásica y Moderna BARRIO
NORTE A restaurant and bar branching out from a vintage bookstore, this cozy brick-walled joint holds everything from poetry readings to dance and live music recitals, including jazz, Latin, tango, piano, and cabaret. Nightly shows at 9:30 or 10pm. *Callao 892.* ☎ *11/4812-8707. Tickets free–AR$25. www.clasicaymoderna.com. Subte: Callao (D). Map p 122.*

★ Estadio Obras Sanitarios
PALERMO An oddball name (Sanitation Works Stadium, anyone?) for a major (5,000-seat) air-conditioned stadium that's home to some of the capital's best hard-rock concerts,

from the Red Hot Chili Peppers to Mötorhead. *Av. del Libertador 7395 (4km northwest of Hipódromo Argentino in Palermo).* ☎ *11/4702-3223. Tickets AR\$25–AR\$60. www. estadioobras.com.ar. Subte: No access.*

★ **Los Cardones** PALERMO VIEJO   A *peña* is a low-key joint with live folkloric music programs, celebrating the traditional song of the Argentine countryside. This appealing *peña* attracts artists from across the country, but particularly the north, where traditions run strong. Gauchos and folks in Buenos Aires for the annual La Rural exhibition in July make Los Cardones their own. *Jorge Luis Borges 2180.* ☎ *11/ 4777-1112. Minimum consumption one drink. www.cardones.com.ar. Subte: Plaza Italia (D). Map p 121.*

★ **Luna Park** CENTRO   The largest indoor stadium in Argentina, hosting big-name pop and rock acts, like Alanis Morissette and the Backstreet Boys, as well as occasional classical music, Julio Bocca's Ballet Argentino, and boxing and other sporting events. *Bouchard 465.*

Polo is a sport with a long-standing history in Argentina.

Luna Park hosts world-class concerts and the esteemed Ballet Argentino.

☎ *11/5279-5279. Tickets AR\$20– AR\$90. www.lunapark.com.ar. Subte: L.N. Alem (B). Map p 122.*

★★ **Thelonious Club** PALERMO A small and stylish upstairs jazz club and cocktail bar, which plays host to fine programs of live modern jazz and hip DJs, operated by two musician brothers. *Salguero 1884.* ☎ *11/ 4829-1562. Minimum consumption one drink. www.theloniousclub.com. ar. Subte: Bulnes (D). Map p 121.*

★★ **La Trastienda** SAN TELMO A medium-sized venue in a late-19th-century mansion that hosts the top alternative and Latin acts, such as Mexico's Café Tacuba and Van Van, from Cuba. *Balcarce 460.* ☎ *11/4342-7650. Tickets AR\$15– AR\$45. www.latrastienda.com. Subte: Plaza de Mayo (A). Map p 122.*

Spectator Sports
★★ **Campo Argentino de Polo** PALERMO   Though the province of the upper classes, polo might still be considered, along with *fútbol*,

The Super Classic

A fútbol match between Buenos Aires's crosstown rivals, Boca Juniors (of working-class La Boca) and River Plate (of upscale Palermo/Núñez) is called a *Superclásico*. It's a much-anticipated matchup, and the city—half decked out in yellow and blue, the other half in black and red—comes to a virtual standstill when the collision goes down.

the national game of Argentina. Opportunities to see it in the capital, however, are limited. The Campo Argentino de Polo is the acclaimed late-19th-century "cathedral of polo," and this is where the annual Abierto de Polo (Open) matches, a tournament with more than a century of history, take place in November. Tickets can be hard to come by. *Av. del Libertador (at Av. Dorrego), Palermo.* ☎ *11/4576-5600 or 11/4777-8005. Tickets AR$25–AR$150. www.aapolo.com. Subte: Plaza Italia (C). Map p 121.*

★★★ Club Atlético Boca Juniors LA BOCA The most

famous *fútbol* (soccer) team in Argentina, the team of Diego Maradona, is Boca, whose yellow-and-blue-clad fans are among the sport's craziest. The monster, vertiginous 1940 stadium Estadio Club Boca Juniors is known to all as La Bombonera (the box of chocolates), and seeing a match here is an unforgettable experience. For the uninitiated, the *platea baja* (seated zone) tickets are best; *popular* is where the crazies congregate, and it may not be safe. **Brandsen 805 (2km south of Plaza Dorrego in San Telmo)**. ☎ *11/4309-4700 or 11/4362-1100. Tickets AR$15–AR$120.*

Estadio Club Boca Juniors, home to some of Argentina's most fanatical soccer fans.

www.bocajuniors.com.ar. Subte: No access. Map p 122.

★★ Club Atlético River Plate

NUNEZ   Boca's crosstown rival is River Plate, known to its fans simply as River (pronounced "ree-ver"). Its fans are equally as passionate, though perhaps a bit less rowdy, at matches held at Estadio Monumental (which hosted the 1978 World Cup and also mega-concerts by artists such as Madonna). *Av. Figueroa Alcorta 7597.* ☎ *11/4788-1200. Tickets AR$20–AR$140. www.cariver plate.com.ar. Subte: No access. Map p 121.*

★★ Hipódromo de Palermo

PALERMO   The stately, historic *hipódromo* (race track) hosts weekly races. On many days, there are few spectators beyond hardcore bettors, but it's a great chance to see the thunderous appeal of Argentine thoroughbreds up close. *Hipódromo: Av. del Libertador 4101, Palermo.* ☎ *11/4778-2839. Free admission. Races Mon & Fri from 3pm; check for additional times. Subte: Plaza Italia (D). Map p 121.*

Tango Shows (tanguerías)

★ Bar Sur SAN TELMO   This cool old corner bar is a mainstay of the bohemian San Telmo neighborhood. It has a surprisingly slick and professional nightly tango dance show, in an intimate environment. *Estados Unidos 299.* ☎ *11/4362-6086. Tickets AR$80–AR$220. www.bar-sur. com.ar. Subte: Independencia (C). Map p 122.*

★ Café La Puerto Rico MONSERRAT   One of the city's most historic cafes (founded in 1887) holds small-scale tango music and occasional dance shows (including flamenco and Arab belly dancing) on Saturday nights, on the charmingly simple stage. *Adolfo Alsina 416.* ☎ *11/4331-2215. Tickets*

AR$10–AR$25. www.lapuertorico cafe.com.ar. Subte: Perú (A) or Bolívar (E). Map p 122.

★★★ Café Tortoni MONSERRAT   A great option for folks wanting to kill two birds with one stone, visiting the city's most famous cafe and seeing a delightful tango show in the back room. The nightly (9pm) shows are unique and high-quality, but not nearly as expensive as the fancier tourist shows. *Av. De Mayo 825.* ☎ *11/4342-4328. Tickets AR$15–AR$30. www.cafetortoni. com.ar. Subte: Piedras (A). Map p 122.*

★ El Querandí MONSERRAT   A 1920s restaurant, El Querandí puts on a very enjoyable show that gives a narrative of the history of the dance and tango culture, from its working-class, sailors-and-bordello roots to the current, sexy "tango-for-export" version. A good dinner-theater show, and the restaurant operates a good little wine bar (La Cava) next door for a pre- or after-show drink. *Perú 302.* ☎ *11/5199-1770. Tickets US$50–US$140. www. querandi.com.ar. Shows Mon–Sat*

The elegant Esquina Carlos Gardel.

Advance Tickets & Listings

For advance tickets of all kinds, including cultural and sports events, contact **Ticketek Argentina** (☎ 11/5237-7200; www. ticketek.com.ar). Current listings of events can be found in the *Buenos Aires Herald* (in English) or *Cultural BA* (a local government free weekly publication, in Spanish).

8:30 & 11:30pm. Subte: Bolívar (E) or Perú (A). Map p 122.

★★ El Viejo Almacén SAN
TELMO   This historic corner colonial-style house hosts one of the most atmospheric places to see a professional *tanguería*. Although slick, they're intimate, pretty traditional in style, and not as glitzy as the big shows. Dinner is offered across the street at Bs As Querido as part of a package. *Balcarce 799 (at Independencia).* ☎ *11/4307-6689. Tickets AR$180–AR$400. www.viejo-almacen.com.ar. Shows nightly 10pm. Subte: Independencia (C). Map p 122.*

★★★ Esquina Carlos Gardel
ABASTO   In the neighborhood of Carlos Gardel (1890–1935), and in

El Viejo Almacén is one of the most atmospheric places to see a professional tanguería.

the 1893 cantina Chanta Cuatro, where Gardel used to hang out, this is one of the best of the flashy *tanguerías*. With a good orchestra, plenty of Gardel songs, excellent dancers, and an elegant stage and salon, even the most jaded *tangueros* should enjoy a show here. Shows are quite a bit more expensive than some of its competitors. *Carlos Gardel 3200.* ☎ *11/4867-6363. Tickets AR$245–AR$700. www.esquinacarlosgardel.com.ar. Shows nightly 9pm. Subte: Carlos Gardel (B). Map p 122.*

★★ Piazzolla Tango CENTRO
This gorgeously restored Belle-Epoque theater is home to a sleek and sophisticated tango show. The opulent surroundings of the palace and its stunning balconies make a real bid for your attention during the show. *Florida 165.* ☎ *11/4344-8201. Tickets AR$180–AR$480. www.piazzollatango.com. Subte: Florida (B). Map p 122.*

★ Señor Tango BARRACAS   This
over-the-top spectacle is rather like the *Miss Saigon* of Broadway-esque tango shows: big, bold, and showy—but most people will have a hard time quibbling with something so well-executed. The top-tier price may be another matter. The show's owner is the star singer. *Vieytes 1655 (3 km south of Parque Lezama).* ☎ *11/4303-0231. Tickets AR$80–AR$600. www.senortango.com.ar. Shows nightly 10:30pm. Subte: No access.* ●

Lodging Best Bets

The Four Seasons is one of the best hotels in the city for families.

Best **Romantic Hotel**
★★★ Legado Mítico $$$ *Gurruchaga 1848 (p 142)*

Best **Business Hotel**
★ Hilton Buenos Aires $$$$ *Av. Macacha Güemes 351 (p 140)*

Best **Cutting-Edge Design**
★★★ Tailor Made Hotel $$ *Arce 385 (p 144)*

Best **Hotel Bar**
★★★ Hotel Home Buenos Aires $$$ *Honduras 5860 (p 141)*; and ★★ Alvear Palace Hotel $$$$ *Av. Alvear 1891 (p 136)*

Best **In-House Restaurant**
★★ Alvear Palace Hotel $$$$ *Av. Alvear 1891 (p 136)*; and ★★★ Bobo Hotel & Restaurant $$$ *Guatemala 4882 (p 136)*

Best **Gay Hotel**
★★ Axel Hotel $$ *Venezuela 649 (p 136)*

Best **Boutique Hotel**
★★★ Hotel Home Buenos Aires $$$ *Honduras 5860 (p 141)*; and ★★★ Costa Petit Hotel $$$ *Costa Rica 5141 (p 138)*; and ★★★ 1555 Malabia House Hotel $$$ *Malabia 1555 (p 139)*

Best **Argentine Theme**
★★ Legado Mítico $$$ *Gurruchaga 184 (p 142)*; and ★★ Gurda Tango Boutique Hotel *Defensa 1521 (p 140)*

Best **Design on a Budget**
★★ The Cocker $ *Juan de Garay 458 (p 137)*

Best **City Views**
★★ Moreno Hotel $$$ *Moreno 376 (p 142)*; and ★ Panamericano Buenos Aires Hotel $$$ *Carlos Pelligrini 551 (p 143)*

Best **for Families**
★★ Four Seasons Hotel Buenos Aires $$$$ *Posadas 1086/88 (p 140)*; and ★★ Gurda Tango Boutique Hotel $ *Defensa 1521 (p 140)*

Best **Value Boutique Hotel**
★★ Krista Hotel Boutique $$ *Bonpland 1665 (p 142)*

Best **Hostel That's a Step Up from a Hostel**
★ Hostel Club V&S $ *Viamonte 887 (p 141)*

Best **Palatial Hotel**
★★★ Palacio Duhau/Park Hyatt Buenos Aires $$$$ *Av. Alvear 1661 (p 143)*

Best **Retro (Deco) Flavor**
★★ Moreno Hotel $$$ *Moreno 376 (p 142)*

Best **Rooftop Pool**
★ Panamericano Buenos Aires Hotel $$$ *Carlos Pelligrini 551 (p 143)*

Centro/San Telmo Lodging

Axel Hotel 9
Castelar Hotel & Spa 6
Esplendor Buenos Aires 3
Faena Hotel + Universe 13
Gurda Tango
  Boutique Hotel 12
Hilton Buenos Aires 14
Hostel Club V&S 2
Hostal Carlos Gardel 10
Moreno Hotel 8
NH City Hotel 7
NH Latino 4
Panamericano Buenos
  Aires Hotel 1
725 Continental Hotel 5
The Cocker 11

Recoleta Lodging

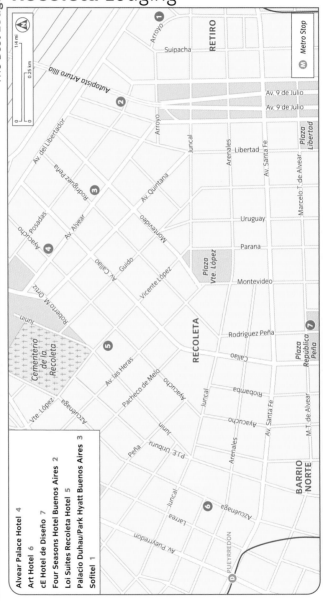

Alvar Palace Hotel 4

Art Hotel 6

cE Hotel de Diseño 7

Four Seasons Hotel Buenos Aires 2

Loi Suites Recoleta Hotel 5

Palacio Duhau/Park Hyatt Buenos Aires 3

Sofitel 1

Palermo Lodging

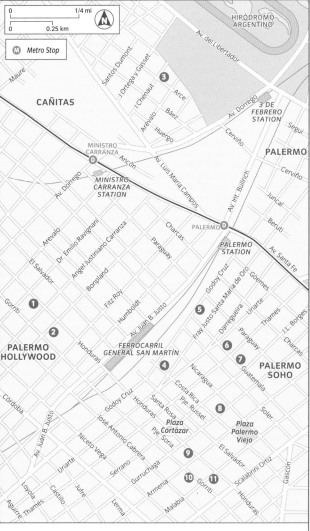

Bobo Hotel & Restaurant 7	1555 Malabia House Hotel 11
Che Lulu Trendy Hotel 5	Five Cool Rooms 9
Costa Petit Hotel 4	Hotel Home Buenos Aires 1
Esplendor Palermo 6	Krista Hotel Boutique 2
Legado Mitico 8	
Mine Hotel Boutique 10	
Tailor Made Hotel 3	

Buenos Aires Hotels A to Z

★★ Alvear Palace Hotel RECO-LETA   The granddaddy of Buenos Aires hotels, with history, class, and location on its side. This 1932 classic is the refuge of presidents, business magnates, and other elite travelers. Rooms are opulent; La Bourgogne is renowned for fine French dining; and service and amenities are formal and top-notch in all respects. The newest addition, the immense La Prairie spa, is the height of luxury. *Av. Alvear 1891.* ☎ *11/4808-2100. www.alvear palace.com. 210 units. US$450– US$600 double, including buffet breakfast. AE, DC, MC, V. Subte: No access. Map p 134.*

Art Hotel RECOLETA   A small, European-style boutique hotel in a century-old townhouse, this place lives up to its name, with a modern-art gallery on the ground floor. The high ceilings and antique elevator speak to the historic nature of the

The entrance to the opulent Alvear Palace Hotel in Recoleta.

place, while cozy, smallish rooms are more modern, with concrete floors and neutral tones. Bathrooms are also small, with showers only. *Azcuénaga 1268.* ☎ *11/4821-4744. www.arthotel.com.ar. 36 units. US$95–US$195 double, including buffet breakfast. AE, MC, V. Subte: Puerreydon (D). Map p 134.*

★★ Axel Hotel SAN TELMO   This stylish gay hotel is a spinoff of the successful model that began in Barcelona and calls itself "hetero-friendly." And while the cool stylings—including outdoor and indoor pools, minimalist rooms, and hipster bar—appeal to gay travelers, it's also great for tolerant travelers of all stripes, even if the location is a bit out of the way. *Venezuela 649.* ☎ *11/4136-9393. www.axel hotels.com. 48 units. US$140– US$170 double. AE, DC, MC, V. Subte: Belgrano (E). Map p 133.*

★★★ Bobo Hotel & Restaurant PALERMO SOHO   Though the name, derived from "bourgeois" and "bohemian," may strike some as the height of pretension, this tiny boutique hotel in a handsome Palermo home is remarkably well-executed, with a great sense of individuality. Each of the seven rooms has its own decorative base based on an art movement: pop, rationalist, Art Deco, and minimalist, among others. The restaurant is superb, so good that you'll surely be tempted to eat more than just a delicious breakfast here. *Guatemala 4882.* ☎ *11/4774-0505. www.bobo hotel.com. 7 units. US$165–US$195 double. AE, DC, MC, V. Subte: No access. Map p 135.*

Castelar Hotel & Spa MONSER-RAT   This 1929 hotel has an illustrious past, hosting the Spanish

The décor at the gay-oriented "heterofriendly" Axel Hotel is chic and modern.

playwright García Lorca (1898–1936) for six months in the 1930s. It remains popular with guests who love Buenos Aires's *cafés notables* and early-20th-century glamour— the hotel, after all, is the work of Mario Palanti (1885–1979), the eccentric Italian architect who built Palacio Barolo—though rooms need some upkeep. The huge, white-marble spa is a major attraction. *Av. de Mayo 1152.* ☎ *11/4383-5000. www.castelarhotel.com.ar. 151 units. AR$450 double, including buffet breakfast. AE, DC, MC, V. Subte: Lima (A). Map p 133.*

kids Che Lulu Trendy Hotel PALERMO SOHO Though complicated to find, this value-oriented little hotel on a quiet Palermo Viejo side street is essentially just a step up from a hostel. Rooms in the bright-red, three-story building aren't large, but they're vibrantly colored and playful. The owners also operate a series of flats, good for families who are economizing. *Pje. Emilio Zolá 5185.* ☎ *11/4772-0289. www.chelulu.com. 8 units.* US$40–US$65 double. MC, V. Subte: No access. Map p 135.*

★★ Ce Hotel de Diseño BARRIO NORTE This smart hotel is committed to its austere, modern design. Spacious rooms, occupying a slender tower, have poured-concrete floors and sleek minimalist furnishings. Several have expansive views from floor-to-ceiling windows over the green square and handsome Ministry of Culture below. Suites are a big step up in space and style. *Marcelo T. Alvear 1695.* ☎ *11/5237-3100. www.designce.com. 28 units. US$150–US$160 double. AE, DC, MC, V. Subte: Callao (D). Map p 134.*

★★ The Cocker SAN TELMO In a still-dodgy section of San Telmo, this British-owned small inn is a wonderful and surprising retreat, loaded with new and old style, and packed with features for the bargain rates. Occupying a brilliantly restored Art Nouveau town house, public rooms are warm and artistic, with cool art, clever touches, and nicely chosen antiques. On the top floor are a delightful garden and

The spacious rooms at Ce Hotel de Diseño feature a minimalist design.

terrace. Each room is wonderfully unique. *Juan de Garay 458.* ☎ *11/4362-8451. www.thecocker.com. 5 units. US$80–US$105 double. No credit cards. Subte: Independencia (C). Map p 133.*

★★★ Costa Petit Hotel PAL-
ERMO SOHO The smallest of Palermo's fashionable boutique hotels, this swank, upscale four-room inn is like a Ralph Lauren ad come to life. With elegant furnishings, antique silver accents, aged mirrors and hardwood floors, and a leafy central courtyard with small pool, this hotel offers exquisite privacy, though it may be too small for some. *Costa Rica 5141.* ☎ *11/4776-8296. www.costapetithotel.com. 4 units. US$200–US$300 double. AE, DC, MC, V. Subte: No access. Map p 135.*

★ Esplendor Buenos Aires
CENTRO A dramatic midsize hotel, the Esplendor occupies a neo-Classical corner building and has wonderfully high ceilings and French doors, and an art-gallery patio. Rooms feature Bertoia steel-mesh chairs combined with rough-hewn wood tables and pale-wood floors. It boasts a stylish restaurant and bar, and is well-located in the center of the action, but it can be noisy. *San Martin 780.* ☎ *11/5256-8000. www.esplendorbuenosaires.com. 51 units. US$205–US$250 double. AE, DC, MC, V. Subte: Florida (B). Map p 133.*

★ Esplendor Palermo PALERMO
SOHO Slightly bigger than many boutique inns, this cool hotel often surpasses them in functionality. Its sleek lounge-bar and rooftop terrace, which sports a modern chimney, are its most unique features, impersonating a trendy night spot. The stylish rooms have space to stretch out, along with handsome patterns, but service and attention to detail can be spotty. *Guatemala 4931.* ☎ *11/5217-5700. www.esplendorpalermo.com. 27 units. US$150 double. AE, DC, MC, V. Subte: No access. Map p 135.*

★★ Faena Hotel + Universe
PUERTO MADERO This pricey hotel wears its design chic on its sleeve and, in every nook of this ultra-glam retreat, the work of Philippe Starck (1949–). There's a distinct touch of Versace-like Edwardian elegance.

Rooms combine classical and modern aesthetics, with white Empire-style furnishings, and deep-red velvet curtains. The experience (there's an "Experience Manager," rather than concierge) and the self-consciousness are all part of the gig. It's a place to see and be seen, and love or hate. *Martha Salotti 445 (Dique 2, Madero Este).* ☎ 11/4010-9000. *www.faenahotelanduniverse.com. 83 units. US$500–US$550 double, including continental breakfast. AE, MC, V. Subte: No access. Map p 133.*

★★★ 1555 Malabia House Hotel
PALERMO SOHO   Inhabiting a beautiful, 111-year-old former convent, this was the first of the city's stylish boutique hotels and remains one of the best. While retaining elements of its former incarnation (including three rooms with private bathroom outside the room), the stylistic makeover is warm, welcoming, and elegant. With abundant natural light and antiques, including art and chandeliers, it's the epitome of good taste. *Malabia 1555.* ☎ 11/4833-2410. *www.malabiahouse.com.ar. 15 units. US$140–US$190 double, including buffet breakfast. AE, DC, MC, V. Subte: No access. Map p 135.*

A Faena Hotel + Universe suite, elegantly designed by Philippe Starck.

★ Five Cool Rooms
PALERMO SOHO   Though the name would indicate a much smaller property (there are actually 17 rooms), this hotel has a young vibe and is most distinguished by its terrific public spaces: an expansive living room–like lobby, garden sitting areas, and huge rooftop terrace. Rooms are by size (S-M-L-XL), even though most are pretty small and the modern decor predictable. *Honduras 4742.*

The rooftop patio at Five Cool Rooms.

The Hilton's reliable comfort comes with easy access to great shopping.

☎ 11/5235-5555. www.fivebuenos
aires.com. 17 units. US$120–US$220
double, including buffet breakfast.
AE, MC, V. Subte: No access. Map
p 135.

★★ **kids** **Four Seasons Hotel
Buenos Aires** RECOLETA This
top-echelon hotel comprises a contemporary tower and the ultra-
exclusive La Mansión, a 1916 French
chateau with 24-hour butler service
and seven swanky suites that have
played host to Madonna and other
celebrities. With its marble floors,
elegant works of art, and top-of-the-
line service, the Four Seasons is the
height of luxury. Unusually for such
an exclusive hotel, it offers a special
menu of amenities for children.
Posadas 1086/88. ☎ 11/4321-1200.
www.fourseasons.com/buenosaires.
165 units. US$395–US$575 double,
including breakfast. AE, DC, MC, V.
Subte: No access. Map p 134.

★★ **kids** **Gurda Tango Boutique Hotel** SAN TELMO This
small gem and value hotel in a traditional San Telmo house has rooms
named for Argentina's greatest hits
(Tango, Malbec, Borges, and Patagonia) and a distinctive Porteño
accent. Rooms are generally large

and cheerful, and the staff delightful.
The hotel sponsors tango music
events and occasional wine tastings
in its cool little wine bar. *Defensa
1521.* ☎ 11/4307-0646. www.gurda
hotel.com. 7 units. US$110–US$170
double, including continental breakfast. MC, V. Subte: Independencia
(C). Map p 133.

★ **kids** **Hilton Buenos Aires**
PUERTO MADERO With its soaring,
seven-story glass-enclosed atrium
lobby, this large contemporary
hotel, with a convention center
overlooking the docks, is the city's
top business hotel. Rooms are large,
with the handsome but generic look
of large international hotels, and the
location offers easy access to downtown and the Microcentro's thriving
commercial zone. Also boasts a fantastic rooftop pool and sundeck. *Av.
Macacha Güemes 351.* ☎ 800/445-
8667 in North America or 11/4891-
0000. www1.hilton.com. 418 units.
US$200–US$330 double. Subte: L.N.
Alem (B). Map p 133.

Hostel Carlos Gardel SAN
TELMO A no-frills hostel with a
dose of bohemian charm. There are
mostly shared rooms (and bathrooms) in the main hostel, although

the owners have opened a second location across the street with ten double rooms (though most are shared bath and not all have air conditioning). A good option for budget travelers wanting privacy. *Carlos Calvo 579.* ☎ *11/4307-2606.* www. *hostelcarlosgardel.com.ar. 16 units. AR$120 double, AR$30 shared rooms per person; including continental breakfast. No credit cards. Subte: Independencia (C). Map p 133.*

★ Hostel Club V&S CENTRO

A real find, this 10-year-old hostel in a handsome 19th-century *casona* is a great option and superb value for budget travelers and students looking for a bit of style to go along with rock-bottom prices. Centrally located, it offers a TV/living area, library, kitchen, terrace, attractive rooms with period details, and air conditioning—and even tango and Spanish lessons. *Viamonte 887.* ☎ *11/4322-0994.* www.hostelclub. *com. US$70–US$73 double, US$13– US$14 shared rooms per person; including continental breakfast. No credit cards. Subte: Lavalle (C). Map p 133.*

★★★ Hotel Home Buenos Aires PALERMO SOHO

A hip Argentine-British couple owns this

The lobby at Hostel Carlos Gardel.

brilliantly styled but warm and comfortable boutique hotel. From the lobby's mid-century Scandinavian furnishings and the gorgeous vintage wallpaper that distinguishes each room to the backyard pool and brand-new spa, it's tough to beat on all accounts, even price. Rooms are warm and chic, with splashes of color, blonde woods, and retro accents. The cool little bar, with DJs that include the owner, is open to non-guests but shuts down by midnight. *Honduras 5860.* ☎ *11/4778-1008.* www.homebuenosaires.com.

Hotel Home Buenos Aires is superbly decorated with modern and vintage pieces.

21 units. US$125–US$175 double, including buffet breakfast. AE, MC, V. Subte: No access. Map p 135.

★★ Krista Hotel Boutique PALERMO HOLLYWOOD In an early-20th-century mansion built around a central courtyard, this intimate and charming small inn has incorporated the house's original elements—moldings, old windows, paneled woodwork, and stylish patterned marble floors—to give it a warm atmosphere. Rooms, most of which are on the ground floor, open onto the courtyard. Krista doesn't try to be hipper than thou, just a well done, romantic retreat—and at a fair price. Bonpland 1665. ☎ 11/4771-4697. www.kristahotel.com.ar. 10 units. US$125–US$160 double, including buffet breakfast. AE, MC, V. Subte: No access. Map p 135.

★★★ Legado Mitico PALERMO SOHO The name refers to the theme of this unique, upscale boutique hotel, highlighting legendary Argentine figures. Thus, you have a Borges room, an Evita room, a Che room—with books, black-and-white photographs, and objects illustrating their legacies. It sounds kitschy, though it's anything but; spacious rooms are sophisticated and romantic, with elegant furnishings and a

Mine Hotel Boutique has an eclectic décor and friendly staff.

relaxed sense of design. There's a beautiful library, fireplace lounge, solarium with hot tub, and leafy patio. Gurruchaga 1848. ☎ 11/4778-1008. www.legadomitico.com. 11 units. US$190–US$280 double, including buffet breakfast. AE, DC, MC, V. Subte: No access. Map p 135.

★ Loi Suites Recoleta Hotel RECOLETA The flagship of a small Argentine chain, this midsize hotel in the heart of an elite neighborhood has warmly contemporary rooms rising 13 floors above Recoleta Cemetery. But the most outstanding feature is a Roman-style, palm- and plant-filled atrium and heated pool under a retractable roof. Studio-style rooms have microwaves, sinks, and small fridges. Vicente López 1955. ☎ 11/5777-8950. www.loisuites.com.ar. 112 units. US$180–US$225 double, including buffet breakfast. AE, DC, MC, V. Subte: No access. Map p 134.

★ Mine Hotel Boutique PALERMO SOHO A friendly, well-managed boutique hotel, this agreeable place is very chic in the public rooms downstairs, but it aims to make guest rooms a little cozier, with colorful Thai and Indian accents to go with the poured-concrete floors. Though that can be a little jarring, it's a great option for those who find strict modern design too austere. The stylish bar and garden pool are very attractive, and the staff are professional and friendly. Gorriti 4770. ☎ 11/4832-1100. www.minehotel.com. 20 units. US$165–US$190 double. AE, DC, MC, V. Subte: No access. Map p 135.

★★ Moreno Hotel MONSERRAT Reveling in Art Deco style, including stained glass and antique elevators, this restored landmark 1929 building has style to burn. Rooms are huge and chic, with a few Deco touches and high ceilings. The fantastic rooftop deck has great city views, a chimney, and common-use Jaccuzzi.

Moreno Hotel, built in 1929, has been beautifully restored and oozes with style.

Going in next door, under the same ownership, will be an Art Deco theater/tango lounge and restaurant. *Moreno 376. ☎ 11/6091-2000. www.morenobuenosaires.com. 39 units. US$95–US$170 double. AE, DC, MC, V. Subte: Bolívar (E). Map p 133.*

★ NH City Hotel MONSERRAT

This Art Deco hotel has plenty of flash, with stunning Deco details, a spectacular rooftop terrace (with a small pool) with views as far as the eye can see, and a terrific in-house Basque restaurant. Rooms are clean and modern, many with amazing city views. Tower rooms are the newest. If you want to be near the Plaza de Mayo, this is your best choice. *Bolívar 160. ☎ 11/4121-6464. www.nh-hotels.com. 370 units. US$130–US$244 double, including buffet breakfast. AE, DC, MC, V. Subte: Bolívar (E) or Plaza de Mayo (A). Map p 133.*

NH Latino CENTRO This modern ten-story hotel, 2 blocks from the Obelisco, is a functional business travelers' hotel, well-equipped and professional, with large, bright rooms; a good onsite restaurant, gym, and sauna; and proximity to the city's financial district. *Suipacha 309. ☎ 11/4321-6700. www.nh-hotels.com. 100 units. US$120–US$$211 double, including buffet*

breakfast. AE, DC, MC, V. Subte: Diagonal Norte (C). Map p 133.

★★★ Palacio Duhau/Park Hyatt Buenos Aires RECOLETA

Incorporating a historic mansion—in this case, a legitimate palace—the new Park Hyatt has catapulted to the top of a very high heap. More modern, but no less luxurious, than its competitors, it combines the stunning 1934 Palacio Duhau, with its gorgeous salons, marble floors, and columns, with the new Posadas building. Rooms have a soothing contemporary sensibility, with a crispness of style not found elsewhere, and unrivalled amenities. *Av. Alvear 1661. ☎ 800/492-8804 in North America or 11/5171-1234. www.buenosaires.park.hyatt.com. 165 units. US$505–US$755 double. AE, DC, MC, V. Subte: No access. Map p 134.*

★ Panamericano Buenos Aires Hotel CENTRO

This high-rise hotel on Av. 9 de Julio packs surprises that elevate it above a tour-group hotel. The interior is stunningly good-looking, with black-and-white marble floors and cool lounges. Then there's the refined restaurant, Tomo I. But the greatest surprise is on the roof: a jaw-dropping, 23rd-floor, glass-enclosed spa, health club, and pool,

NH City Hotel, near the Plaza de Mayo, is elegantly styled with Art Deco accents.

The Panamericano Buenos Aires Hotel features black-and-white marble floors.

with arresting 360-degree views of the Obelisco and city. Service gets panned, though. *Carlos Pelligrini 551.* ☎ *11/4348-5000. www.panamericano.us. 360 units. US$315–US$350 double, including buffet breakfast. AE, DC, MC, V. Subte: Lavalle, Diagonal Norte (C). Map p 133.*

★ 725 Continental Hotel

RETIRO This is one of the more unexpected large hotels in town; housed in an iconic, hexagonal 1927 Alejandro Bustillo building in a congested section of the Centro, it is all about cool, refined modern style, with classic mid-century pieces and vibrant colors throughout. The hotel has a rooftop bar and small outdoor, heated swimming pool, but may be a bit overpriced. *Av. Saenz Peña 725.* ☎ *866/376-7831 in North America or 11/4131-8000. www.epoquehotels.com. 192 units. US$260–US$$460 double, including breakfast. AE, MC, V. Subte: Diagonal Norte (C). Map p 133.*

★★ Sofitel RETIRO This superlative five-star French hotel on a quiet street lined with art galleries is one

of the city's finest and most prestigious. Opened in 2003, it has a glass-enclosed lobby that joins two buildings with the landmark 1929 Art Deco Mihanovich tower. The stately rooms are an elegant mix of classic French and Deco accents, with gorgeous marble bathrooms. Service is impeccable. *Arroyo 841/849.* ☎ *11/4131-0000. www.sofitel buenosaires.com.ar. 144 units. US$510–US$535 double. AE, DC, MC, V. Subte: San Martin. Map p 134.*

★★★ Tailor Made Hotel LAS

CANITAS Amid the noisy bars and restaurants of Las Cañitas, this sleek, modern boutique hotel confidently proposes a monochromatic aesthetic, reinforced by iMacs in rooms and top-quality linens and objects. The five rooms have a Zen-like austerity, with light-wood floors and barren white walls. A unique feature is that laundry, the snack bar, and even international calls are all free. *Arce 385.* ☎ *11/4774-9620. www.tailormadehotels.com.ar. 5 units. US$210–US$250 double, including breakfast. AE, MC, V. Subte: No access. Map p 135.* ●

The glass-enclosed lobby at the five-star Sofitel.

El Tigre & the River Delta

1. Tren de la Costa
2. San Isidro
3. Barrancas (Estación del Anticuario)
4. Parque de la Costa
5. Paseo Victorica
6. Heladería Vía Toscana
7. Museo de Arte Tigre
8. María Luján
9. Delta river tours

Previous page: An old car outside El Drugstore café and bar.

Just an hour's train ride past the city's northern suburbs, the Río de la Plata becomes an immense waterway comprising thousands of miles of rivers, canals, streams, and hundreds of islands and marshlands. An escape for wealthy Porteños since the late 19th century, Tigre is a relaxing place to enjoy a lunch at a riverside restaurant or cruise on the river. If you enjoy kayaking and nature trails, staying at a lodge on one of the Delta islands is a unique experience. On weekends, the area is packed with Porteño families. START: **Subte (C) to Retiro and train to Olivos (Estación Mitre); cross over to Estación Maipú for the Tren de la Costa.**

① ★★ kids **Tren de la Costa.** Although there's a faster, direct train to Tigre from Buenos Aires's Retiro station, I much prefer the charming coastal train, which requires one change in Olivos (at Estación Mitre; cross the overpass to Estación Maipú); from there, it covers just 16km (10 miles) in 25 minutes and 11 stations to the final stop, Delta, in Tigre. You can get off and on the train at stops along the way; each stop has been designed with its own identity, including shops, cafes, and artistic themes targeting passengers (Borges station has a literary cafe; Anchorena is the "Tango station"; and San Isidro has an outdoor mall with pubs and restaurants). ⏱ *45 min. Estación Retiro: Av. Ramos Mejía, 1358.* ☎ *11/4002-6000; www.trendelacosta.com.ar. Admission: AR$16 adults round-trip. Mon–Fri 7:10am–11:25pm; Sat & Sun 8:30am–12:35am.*

② ★★ **San Isidro.** This well-to-do bedroom community is home to many boating and private-club enthusiasts who fled Buenos Aires to raise families. In addition to upscale restaurants and shopping, San Isidro has some important 18th- and

Estación del Anticuario has a café and weekend antiques fair.

Practical Matters: Tigre

The Tigre Tourist Office is located at Estación Fluvial, or Tigre Boat Terminal, no. 1648 (☎ 11/4512-4497; open daily 9am–5pm). **Lodging:** Some 60 hotels and lodges are sprinkled throughout the Delta, up to an hour by boat from Tigre. Among the best options are **Rumbo 90 Delta Lodge & Spa** (☎ 15/5843-9454; www.rumbo90.com.ar), a swank riverfront lodge with six luxury suites, a swimming pool, full spa, restaurant, and all-inclusive rates (starting at US$250); and **La Becasina Delta Lodge** (☎ 11/4328-2687; www.labecasina.com), a charming, rustic 15-room inn on its own island. The all-wood rooms at La Becasina are bungalow-style, and the place has the feel of a jungle lodge, with plenty of outdoor activities, including kayaks (all-inclusive rates start at US$175 per person).

19th-century landmarks, including the 1708 **Cathedral** (on Calle Menini), **Jockey Club** (one of Argentina's two most prestigious polo clubs), and the elegant 1935 **Hipódromo de San Isidro** (horse racing track). Antiques dealers often take over the central square on weekends.

3 ★ **kids** **Barrancas (Estación del Anticuario).** At this retro-flavored train stop, there's a cute cafe (Bike & Coffee) occupying the wood station and a multi-dealer antiques fair up and down the tracks on weekends. The market is a mini-San Telmo fair. The cafe has good coffees, pastries, and simple lunch fair, including soups. *Juan Diaz de Solis 736. $.*

4 ★ **kids** **Parque de la Costa.** Right across from the Delta train station, this old-school amusement park is a charming throwback, with a Big Wheel, wooden roller coasters, boat rides, and colorful "dancing" fountains. *Vivanco 1509.* ☎ *11/4002-6000. www.parquedelacosta.com.ar. Admission: AR$30. Fri–Sun 11am–9pm.*

5 ★★ **kids** **Paseo Victorica.** This pretty riverfront promenade is lined with landscaped gardens and

what remain of the grand, late-19th- and early-20th-century Victorian mansions that once fronted the river. Today, the promenade is a favorite place for leisurely strolls, sipping *mate,* and picnicking. On the bank of the river is the 1876 **Club de la Marina** rowing club.

Paseo Victorica is a great place for a riverside stroll.

Boat cruises are a popular way to explore the river delta.

6 ★★ kids Heladería Vía Toscana. This wonderful little ice cream shop serves some of the best artisanal sorbets and gelatti I've had in Argentina. The passion fruit and peach flavors I tried seemed to have more fruit flavor than the fruits themselves. *Paseo Victorica 470.* ☎ *11/4749-2972. $.*

7 ★★★ Museo de Arte Tigre. Back in its heyday, when Tigre was a refuge for well-dressed aristocrats, this splendid 1910 mansion was its social center: first as the Tigre Club and then the Casino de Tigre. After many years, it has been magnificently restored and repurposed as the Tigre Museum of Art. The collection focuses on some of the biggest names in Argentine figurative art from the 19th and 20th centuries. Although it's not hard to imagine elegant aristocrats of the day climbing the grand staircase, period photographs downstairs will help you recreate the ambience. ⏱ *1 hr. Paseo Victorica 972.* ☎ *11/4512-4528. www.vivitigre.gov. ar. Admission: AR$5 adults. Wed–Fri 9am–7pm; Sat & Sun noon–7pm. Free guided visits (in Spanish): Wed–Fri 11am & 4pm; Sat & Sun 1, 3 & 5pm.*

8 ★★ María Luján. Tigre's best bet for lunch or dinner is this handsome restaurant, in an 1890 casona with a terrace overlooking the Luján river. On sunny afternoons, it's the place to be, and getting a table on weekends can be a challenge. It serves excellent salads and seafood, as well as homemade pastas and *parrillada. Paseo Victorica 611.* ☎ *11/ 4731-9613. www.ilnovomariadellujan. com. $$$.*

9 ★★★ kids Delta river tours. One of the highlights of the Delta is taking a river cruise on a *lancha* that traverses the rivers Luján, Sarmiento, and San Antonio, as well as some smaller canals, passing or even stopping at some of the islands. *Paseos* on catamarans and larger boats depart from the Estación Fluvial (Av. General Mitre, s/n) and range from AR$15 to AR$35 for hour or 90-minute trips. The tourism office has a list of operators, which can also be viewed at: www.tigre.gov.ar. More intrepid visitors can also hire canoes, kayaks, and rowboats.

Uruguay: Colonia del Sacramento

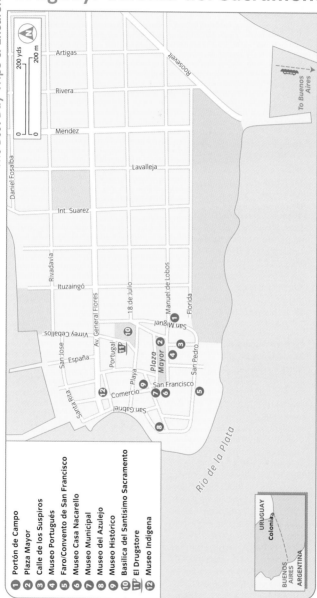

1. Portón de Campo
2. Plaza Mayor
3. Calle de los Suspiros
4. Museo Portugués
5. Faro/Convento de San Francisco
6. Museo Casa Nacarello
7. Museo Municipal
8. Museo del Azulejo
9. Museo Histórico
10. Basílica del Santísimo Sacramento
11. El Drugstore
12. Museo Indígena

A popular day or overnight trip for visitors to Buenos Aires isn't in Argentina at all—but just one hour by high-speed ferry in its northern neighbor, Uruguay. Colonia del Sacramento is a charming colonial town, a former Portuguese settlement dating to 1680 and a UNESCO World Heritage site. The Barrio Histórico's colorful houses, pristine cobblestoned streets, and seven small historic museums—alongside pleasant cafes, restaurants, shops, and bars—are contained within the remains of its ancient stone walls. START: **Ferry to Colonia from Puerto Madero (ferries either 1 or 3 hours).**

❶ ★ **Portón de Campo.** Crossing a drawbridge to the original 1745 stone gate, at the far southwestern corner of town, is the best way to enter the Barrio Histórico. Most of the original stone ramparts, dating to 1639, that encircled the defensive outpost of Colonia were destroyed in the 19th century. *Calle Manuel Lobo at Calle de San Miguel.*

❷ ★ **Plaza Mayor.** The pretty, tree-lined town square was the heart of the Portuguese colonial settlement here in 1680. *Calle de San Antonio.*

❸ ★★★ **Calle de los Suspiros.** Colonia's most photogenic street, lined with faded one-story pastel houses with tile roofs, and jagged, uneven stone pavement, has a unique past, alluded to in its poetic name. According to some, "The

"The Street of Sighs" is lined with faded, pastel houses.

Street of Sighs" refers to the days when sailors would dock in Colonia and visit their girlfriends here. A competing legend claims, less romantically, that soldiers were executed at the end of the street, spilling their blood and expending their last breaths. *Between Calle San Pedro and Plaza Mayor.*

❹ ★ **Museo Portugués.** A 1720 Portuguese construction with original walls and flooring features exhibits of Portuguese weapons, clothing, and ceramics, giving a sense of Colonia's beginnings. The interior (of stone, wood, and tile) is particularly attractive. The annex to the original house is Spanish, dating from the end of the 18th century. This collection and the other small museums nearby will mainly be attractive to those with an interest in colonial history, though the homes themselves are worth a look. *Plaza Mayor (between Calles de Solís and de los Suspiros). Admission: Museum (UR$50) valid for eight museums).*

❺ **Faro/Convento de San Francisco.** Jesuits and Franciscans established a convent in Colonia shortly after the settlement's founding toward the end of the 17th century, part of their efforts to teach and convert indigenous peoples in the Americas. The Jesuits founded a school here in 1717, but it, like the convent, lies in ruins. Next to it is the gleaming white *faro*, the old but

Colonia's Rich History

Colonia was an important strategic defense point in the trade of contraband and West African slaves, first controlled by the Portuguese on their way to Brazil, and then by the Spanish (changing hands back and forth eight times through the early 19th century). The settlement's curious origins are addressed in the circuit of museums in the Barrio Histórico. A museum circuit might sound daunting for a day trip, but the museums are tiny—they can all be visited on foot in just a couple of hours and are most interesting for the houses themselves. For most people, the greatest pleasure in visiting Colonia is wandering its delightful old streets, taking in its Portuguese and Spanish stucco architecture, and the fragrant flowers adorning nearly every street.

still functioning lighthouse. *Calle de San Francisco (between Plaza Mayor & Calle de San Pedro).*

⑥ **Museo Casa Nacarello.** This mid-18th-century house conserves its original stone walls and is worth a quick visit to see the original layout of a period Portuguese house. *Calle del Comercio 67 (Plaza Mayor). Admission: Museum (UR$50) valid for eight museums.*

El Drugstore has a daily menu and Spanish tapas.

⑦ ★ **Museo Municipal (Casa de Almirante Brown).** The municipal museum, occupying a house said to have belonged to the Irishman Admiral Guillermo Brown (who played a pivotal role in Uruguay's independence), exhibits historical documents about the town, maps, colonial furniture, and religious relics, as well as archaeological and paleontological artifacts. *Calle del Comercio 77. Admission: Museum (UR$50) valid for eight museums.*

⑧ ★ **Museo del Azulejo.** This tiny, restored 18th-century Portuguese country house (walls, some beams, and parts of the floor are original) displays 300-year-old Portuguese, Catalan, French, and Uruguayan glazed ceramic tiles, or *azulejos*. *Calle Misiones de los Tapes 104 (at Paseo San Gabriel). Admission: Museum (UR$50) valid for eight museums.*

⑨ **Museo Histórico (Casa Palacios).** A 1750 Portuguese house that belonged to the Palacios family has many original components and today houses a collection of regional archives, including old city maps and police files. *Misiones de los Tapes at Calle del Comercio.*

Admission: Museum (UR$50) valid for eight museums.

⑩ Basílica del Santísimo Sacramento. This handsomely weathered church, with worn white bricks, is the oldest in Uruguay, dating to Colonia's founding in 1680. The austere interior is an excellent example of 17th-century colonial religious architecture. *Calle Vasconcelos, s/n.*

⑪ ★ kids El Drugstore. A popular and cheery, bohemian-feeling restaurant and bar, with outdoor tables near old cars parked outside. It's directly across from the Basílica and serves up a daily menu and Spanish tapas, along with regular live music, from reggae to flamenco. *Portugal 174.* ☎ *052/25241. $$.*

⑫ Museo Indígena. Housed in a 19th-century Spanish home is the private collection of items—including knives, arrowheads, and mortars—once belonging to the indigenous Charruas Indians who inhabited the area. *Calle General Flores 327. Admission: Museum (UR$50) valid for eight museums.*

Practical Matters: Colonia

Buquebus (☎ 11/4316-6500; www.buquebus.com) has at least two high-speed ferries departing from Av. Antártida Argentina 821 (Dique 4) in Buenos Aires to Colonia, 8:45 and 11:30am daily, for the 1-hour trip (AR$200–AR$250 roundtrip adults); advance deals available online. The regular ferry takes 3 hours ($AR124–AR$181 roundtrip adults). A newer ferry service, slightly cheaper than Buquebus's 1-hr ferry (AR$168–AR$224 roundtrip adults) and with fewer departures is **Colonia Express** (Av. Pedro de Mendoza 33; ☎ 11/4317-4100; www.coloniaexpress.com).

Visas and currency: Passports are required for travel, but citizens of Canada, New Zealand, Australia, and South Africa have joined citizens of the United States and the United Kingdom in no longer needing visas for entry. The Uruguayan peso is the official currency, but every business in Colonia accepts payment in Argentine pesos and U.S. dollars, as well. There's a helpful **tourist information office** just outside the Portón de Campo (gate), open daily from 8am to 8pm; additional information is available at ☎ 052/ 25599, or www.colonia.gub.uy and www.museoscolonia.blogspot. com. Guided walking tours of the Barrio Histórico (US$100 per person) are available Thursday to Sunday at 11am and Monday to Saturday at 3pm. Call ☎ 052/22309. A **museum pass** (UR$50, valid for eight museums) can be purchased at any of the museums on the circuit; tickets for individual museums can not be purchased. Information and a map is available at the Tourist Information Office (just outside the Portón de Campo at the entrance to the old town). Museums are open daily from 11:15am to 4:45pm.

Addresses: Some street addresses here do not have a street number, denoted by s/n (Spanish for "sin nombre", or "without number").

San Antonio de Areco: Gaucho Country

1 Plaza Ruiz de Arellano
2 Parroquia San Antonio de Padua
3 Patricio Draghi
4 Esquina de Merti
5 Museo de Platería Draghi
6 La Belle Epoque
7 Gustavo Stagnaro Platería
8 Almacén Los Principios
9 Puente Viejo
10 Parque Criollo/Museo Ricardo Güiraldes
11 La Cervecería (Old Town Brew)

0   200 yds
0   200 m

The flat pampas (grasslands) radiating outward from Buenos Aires are famous for their unending horizons, *estancias* (ranches), and gaucho culture. For a taste of the Argentine version of the Old West, you need only venture 90 minutes (113km/70 miles) north of the city to San Antonio de Areco, the epicenter of local gaucho traditions. The graceful country town makes an easy day trip, although using one of the nearby *estancias* in the surrounding pampas countryside as a base is also a great option. START: **Driving (by car) from Buenos Aires, take Ruta Nacional 8 north; driving time is about 90 minutes. Buses (2 hours) leave from Terminal de Ómnibus de Retiro (Av. Antártida Argentina at Calle 10).**

❶ ★ Plaza Ruiz de Arellano.
The main square, lined with tall sycamore trees and surrounded by gentle cobblestone streets, is central to life in San Antonio. Beret-topped gauchos and local families gather on benches, drink *mate,* and watch the town's peaceful world go by (which means folks passing slowly on bike, cowboys on horseback, and dogs chasing occasional cars). *Arellano at Mitre.*

❷ ★★ Parroquia San Antonio de Padua. On the south side of Plaza Arellano, the town's main church, its namesake, dates to San Antonio's founding in 1730. What you see today is a late 19th-century rebuilding, so within the colonial

The town's main church was rebuilt in the late 19th century.

Sycamore trees line Plaza Ruiz de Arellano.

Patricio Draghi makes unique jewelery pieces before your eyes.

exterior is a handsome mix of Baroque and Neoclassical elements, with a coffered ceiling and beautiful tiled floor. *Plaza Arellano, s/n.*

❸ ★ Patricio Draghi. One of the top silver shops in town, run by one of the sons of a local silversmithing dynasty. Watch artisans work in the back room, just past an enormous cut-glass chandelier, making superb knives and unique jewelry pieces. *Arellano 45.* ☎ *23/2645-2961.*

❹ ★★★ kids Esquina de Merti. This great-looking bar and restaurant, inhabiting an old *pulpería* (general store), looks like it's been around forever, with its black-and-white tiled floors, worn wooden tables and chairs, antique cash register, and shelves lined with ceramic milk bottles, jars, and thermoses. It's a great lunch stop, with huge and inexpensive portions of *parrillada* (barbecued meats) from the grill in the courtyard, excellent salads, homemade pastas, and tasty empanadas. *Arellano 147.* ☎ *23/2645-6705. $$.*

❺ ★★ kids Museo de Platería Draghi. Although this museum largely functions as an advertisement for the exquisite silver wares of Juan José Draghi, the most recognized silversmith in San Antonio, it offers an intimate view of a master artisan and his traditional craft. The handsome circa-1900 *casona* has a gorgeous stained-glass skylight and, out back, a courtyard and fountain, next to a family-owned small inn. *Lavalle 387.* ☎ *23/2645-4219. www. draghiplaterosorfebres.com. Admission: AR$5 adults. Daily 10am–5pm.*

Esquina de Merti has kept the look of an old general store.

Estancias near San Antonio de Areco

Several traditional working ranches, or *estancias*, within easy reach of SAA have been transformed into rustic lodges and hotels, where guests dabble in gaucho life, eating ***parrilladas***, riding horses, and checking out a polo match or two. The following are three of the best estancias for an overnight stay:

★★ **El Ombú de Areco** This small (nine-room), traditional family-owned estate, has a main house constructed in the style of an Italian villa. The property is full of large, old trees and remains a working ranch, with more than 300 hectares (741 acres) of land, and some 400 cows and other animals. Rooms—with ceiling fans only—have high ceilings and rustic touches. *10km (6¼ miles) from San Antonio de Areco.* ☎ *23/2649-2080* or ☎ *11/4737-0436 in Buenos Aires. www.*

El Ombú de Areco is a family-owned estancia originally built in 1880.

estanciaelombu.com. From US$310 double, including all meals & drinks; US$65 day rate (no overnight stay) includes lunch.

★★ **El Rosario de Areco** This growing family *estancia* is a friendly and down-to-earth place. The origins of the colonial-style ranch—long involved in the breeding of polo horses—date to the late 19th century, and the rooms, in squat terracotta-colored buildings, occupy former horse stalls. You'll find cozy public rooms with a fireplace, a polo field (and polo demonstrations), horseback riding, and two pools. *7km (4¼ miles) from San Antonio de Areco.* ☎ *914/220-7883 in the U.S. or 32/2645-1000. www.rosariodeareco.com.ar. 18 units. From US$215 double, including all meals & drinks; US$70 day rate includes lunch.*

★★★ **La Bamba** A historic and traditional colonial ranch on 150 hectares (371 acres) has a unique past: In 1830, it served as a stage-coach, or post house, stop along the Camino Real from Buenos Aires. One of the first *estancias* to welcome tourists, it has been featured in several films and had the honor of hosting the legendary Carlos Gardel. The rooms (some of which are air-conditioned) in the deep-red main house are romantically decorated, with antique bed and other furniture. Activities include swimming, horseback riding, carriage riding, and massages, and there are occasional gaucho performances at the onsite ***pulpería*** (former general store-cum-tavern). *13km (8 miles) from San Antonio.* ☎ *23/2645-6293. www.la-bamba.com.ar. 12 units. From US$300 double, including all meals & drinks; US$73 day rate includes lunch.*

La Belle Epoque is a chocolate shop that also has excellent gelato.

6 ★ **kids La Belle Epoque.** Chocoholics take note: There are a couple of excellent chocolate shops in town. And though La Olla de Cobre (Matheu 433; ☎ 23/2645-3105) is fantastic and locally famous (and probably tops for chocolate and local specialties turrón and alfajores), this one's adorable and also serves wonderful gelato (of which, logically, the chocolate is outstanding). *Arellano 82.* ☎ *3235/1540-7038. $.*

7 ★★ **Gustavo Stagnaro Platería.** There's no shortage of nice shops with gaucho-related goods

Gustavo Stagnora Plateria has excellent silverware and gaucho accessories.

in San Antonio. But this silversmith's boutique is one of the best; in addition to handmade and antique *criollo* silverware, it stocks excellent tapestries and other gaucho culture accessories, such as belts, saddles, and blankets. And the early-19th century casona the shop is housed in is lovely in itself. *Arellano (at Matheu).* ☎ *02326/454-801.*

8 ★★ **Almacén Los Principios.** This old country store, with weathered bricks that wrap around its corner location, looks like a movie set, with an antique scale and shelves stretching to the ceiling and stocked with bottled and canned goods accessible only by ladder. The shop appears not to have changed in nearly a century, and some of the patrons hanging out at the bar look like they may have grown up in the place. The original owner, Don Ferández, is still behind the counter. *Bartolomé Mitre 151 (corner of Moreno).*

9 **Puente Viejo.** In Parque San Martín, the park just north of the main square, the old bridge—once a toll crossing in the 19th century—stretches over the Río Areco that divides the main part of town from its more rural section of parks. The bridge may date to1857 and be a National Historic Landmark, but its refurbishment sadly sapped it of character. You may stare at it and wonder: Can that really be the bridge everyone in town talks about?

10 ★★ **Parque Criollo/Museo Ricardo Güiraldes.** San Antonio's gaucho culture and citizens of the pampas were immortalized in the 1926 novel *Don Segundo Sombra,* an Argentine classic written and set in San Antonio de Areco, and the first significant work to treat gaucho life. This "Museum of the Gaucho" is named for its author

Almacén Los Principios seems as if it hasn't changed in a century.

(who died the year after publication of the work that would make him famous). The colonial hacienda-style museum, inaugurated in 1936, has lovely grounds and incorporates the 1830 Pulpería La Blanqueada, a general store featured in key scenes in the novel. In addition to photographs of characters in the book, the author's personal effects, and gaucho memorabilia, you'll find the kitschy oddity of gaucho mannequins welcoming you to the museum's exhibit rooms. *Camino Ricardo Güiraldes (Parque Criollo).*

☎ 23/2645-5839. Admission: AR$4 adults. Wed–Mon 11am–5pm.

🍺 ★ **La Cerveceria (Old Town Brew).** Highly unusual in Argentina, this cool brew pub makes five varieties of its own artisanal beers, including a pilsner, pale ale, and porter. All are perfect for washing down the gourmet pizzas, sandwiches, and snacks. *Zapiola, 76 (between Matheu and Lavalle).* ☎ 02326/456-408. $. Tues–Sat 6:30–11; Sun, noon–9pm.

The Gauchos' Traditional Celebration

San Antonio de Areco celebrates its traditions and gaucho culture during the annual **Día de la Tradición,** which, despite the name, is actually stretched into a week or more, held around the 10th of November. The entire town is taken over by gauchos (and their horses) in their finest duds, participating in parades, folkloric music and dance, and *criollo* skill demonstrations and competitions, such as the *sortija,* which involves catching rings while on horseback (later used to woo the local women). San Antonio's few hotels book solid for the celebration, so plan in advance if you want to come in early November.

A typical street in San Antonio de Areco.

Practical Matters: San Antonio de Areco

By car from Buenos Aires, drive north on Ruta Nacional 8. The drive takes about 90 minutes. By bus (about 2 hr., US$8 roundtrip adults): **Nueva Chevallier** (☎ 11/4000-5255; www.nuevachevallier. com) offers frequent bus service from Retiro Bus Terminal. Reserve ahead in summer and for weekend travel. You'll find a **tourist information office** in Parque San Martín (Av. Zerboni at Arellano), open daily 8am to 7pm; ☎ 23/2645-3165; sanantoniodeareco.com/ turismo.

Lodging: The top hotel in town is the luxurious boutique hotel **Patio de Moreno** (Moreno 215; ☎ 23/2645-5144; www.patiode moreno.com; US$120–US$180 double), a new and handsomely restored old build- ing with six extremely well-appointed, contemporary rooms, just 4 blocks from Plaza Arellano. **Draghi Para- dores** (Lavalle 387; ☎ 23/2645- 5583; www.sanantoniodeareco. com/paradores; US$75 double), is nearly as comfortable, a colonial- style, five-room inn directly behind the Draghi museum, with attrac- tively rustic rooms, a small pool and fountain, and free bicycle use. ●

Patio de Moreno is the top hotel in town.

The
Savvy Traveler

Subte

Before You Go

Government Tourist Offices

IN CANADA   Consulate General of Argentina, 2000 Peel St., Suite 600, Montreal, Quebec H3A 2W5 (☎ 514/842-6582; www.consargenmtl.com).

IN THE U.S.   The Argentina Government Tourist Office, 12 W. 56th St., New York, NY 10019 (☎ 212/603-0443; www.turismo.gov.ar); and 2655 Le Jeune Rd., PH1, Suite F, Coral Gables, FL 33134 (☎ 305/442-1366).

IN THE U.K.   Embassy of the Argentine Republic, 65 Brooke St., London W1Y 4AH (☎ 0207/318-1300; www.argentine-embassy-uk.org).

The Best Time to Go

Seasons in Argentina are the opposite of the Northern Hemisphere. The best times to visit Buenos Aires are spring (Sept–Nov) and fall (Mar–May). Spring is particularly nice; during October and November, jacaranda trees bloom across the city, Porteños take to the parks, and the annual Polo Championships comes to town. Beginning in late December, the city becomes quite hot and humid; January and February, the height of summer, are particularly tortuous (with temperatures reaching 38°C/100°F or more), though some may find it a pleasant change from frigid temperatures in the Northern Hemisphere. The city feels a little empty at this time, as those who can head to beach resorts in Mar del Plata or Uruguay. January is also problematic because many restaurants and places of interest either follow limited schedules or close entirely. Winter (June–Aug) isn't impossibly cold, though the city is largely gray and chilly—probably not the best time to see Buenos Aires at its most exuberant.

Previous page: A subway station entrance.

Festivals & Special Events

SPRING   The annual Festival Internacional de Buenos Aires is a 2-week schedule of international theater programs held in late September or early October (☎ 11/4374-2829; www.festivaldeteatroba.gov.ar). Casa FOA (www.casafoa.com), a designers' showcase of home furnishings and decor, takes over an old space and recycles it; every year, it moves someplace new (in recent years, it has been at railroad warehouses and Tigre's Puerto de Frutos). Día de la Tradición (☎ 23/2645-3165; www.sanantonio deareco.com/turismo/fiesta delatradicion) is the annual gaucho celebration in San Antonio de Areco; despite the name, it's a week's worth of photogenic gaucho festivities, skill contests, folk music, and dance. The world's biggest polo event and the fifth-oldest polo tournament in the world, the Abierto Argentino de Polo, is held at the polo grounds in Palermo from mid-November to mid-December (☎ 11/4343-0972; www.aapolo.com).

SUMMER   December 24 holds more importance than Christmas Day, and the biggest event is Noche Buena (Christmas Eve), celebrated with fireworks and much partying. Midnight Mass at the Catedral Metropolitana is the most traditional religious ceremony, a lovely event. Año Nuevo (New Year's Day) is celebrated, as it is in much of the world, with more fireworks and drinking. Buenos Aires isn't Rio, but its version of Carnaval, Fiesta de las Murgas, is celebrated every weekend in February, with band competitions and dancing. Chinese New Year is celebrated in late January or early February, concentrated in Belgrano's

Barrio Chino, with Chinese food and a dragon-blessing parade.

FALL Buenos Aires's important Feria del Libro (Book Festival), one of the largest book festivals in the world, is celebrated for three weeks, from late April to mid-May, at La Rural (www.el-libro.org.ar). Arte BA, a 5-day art fair in late May at La Rural in Palermo, is the largest showing in Argentina of contemporary and young artists (www.arteba.org).

WINTER The Mundial de Tango (World Tango Festival) is celebrated for 10 days at the end of August—with tango dance events, concerts, films, and contests—at La Rural in Palermo and tango salons throughout the city (www.mundialdetango.gov.ar). Día de la Independencia, a national holiday, is celebrated July 9, with cafes on Av. de Mayo marking the occasion of national independence with breakfasts of chocolate con churros. La Rural is the important 2-week agricultural fair, held in Palermo from the end of July to early August at the La Rural Stadium (☎ 11/4324-4700; www.exposicionrural.com.ar); in addition to livestock showings, there are gaucho stunts and contests.

The Weather

Buenos Aires is mostly temperate and mild year-round, without huge extremes except for January and February, which can be forbiddingly hot—often in the high 90s to more than 35°C–40°C (100°F). Summer is also very humid. Winter (July–Oct) gets chilly, but not especially cold (frosts are rare, snow unheard of). Rains are most frequent in autumn and spring (Mar–June and Sept–Dec), though they are generally short.

Cellphones (Celulares; Teléfonos Móviles)

World phones—or GSM (Global System for Mobiles)—work in Argentina (and most of the world). If your cellphone is on a GSM system, and you have a world-capable multiband phone, you can make and receive calls from Argentina. Just call your wireless operator and ask for "international roaming" to be activated. You can also rent a GSM phone. Several companies offer cellphone rentals for Argentina, including Cellular Abroad (www.cellularabroad.com); Alojargentina (www.alojargentina.com.ar); Altel (☎ 800/768-9936; www.altel.com.ar); 4rent Argentina (www.4rentargentina.com/buenos-aires-cell-phone-rental.html); Alquiler de Celulares en Argentina (www.alquiler-celulares.com.ar), and Cellhire (www.cellhire.com/content/cell-phone-argentina.htm).

Car Rentals

If you're planning to stay exclusively in Buenos Aires, there's little or no reason to rent a car. The only reason for a rental car would be for excursions to Tigre and the River Delta (though it's well served by a tourist train) or San Antonio de Areco and the nearby estancias. Driving in the city of Buenos Aires isn't for the faint of heart; besides the expected traffic and parking difficulties of an 11-million-person metropolis, most Porteños appear to believe rules of the road, well, don't apply to them. Traveling by *subte* (subway), taxi, or *remise* (licensed minicab) is much more convenient and safer (and less expensive) than driving. Car rentals are expensive, generally from US$50 to US$75 per day. Among car-rental agencies are Avis, Cerrito 1527 (☎ 800/331-1212 in the U.S. and Canada, or 11/4326-5542; www.avis.com.ar); Baires Rent a

Useful Websites

www.bue.gov.ar The municipal government's comprehensive tourism site with details on neighborhoods and attractions in English as well as Spanish (and Portuguese). Takes some navigating skills.

www.guiaoleo.com.ar The most comprehensive restaurant guide, with user reviews (in Spanish).

www.letstango.com.ar Tango information, *milonga* schedules, and interesting articles on the city and its culture.

www.subte.com.ar Everything you ever wanted to know about the Buenos Aires subway. Good for downloadable maps and schedules.

www.turismo.gov.ar Ministry of Tourism site with travel information for Buenos Aires and the rest of Argentina, though it's largely background information, with less emphasis on practical tips.

www.welcomeargentina.com General country-wide information, with plenty on activities in Buenos Aires.

Car, at Ezeiza International Airport (☎ 11/4822-7361; www.bairesrentacar.com.ar); Budget, San Martín 1225 (☎ 800/472-3325 or 11/4314-7773; www.budget.com.ar); Hertz Annie Millet, Paraguay 1138 (☎ 800/654-3131 or 11/4815-6789; www.milletrentacar.com.ar); and Thrifty, Honduras 4154, Palermo (☎ 800/847-4389 or 810/999- 8500; www.thrifty.com). Gasoline (petrol) is called nafta; diesel is gasoil or diesel; and unleaded gas is sin plomo.

Getting **There**

By Plane

Argentina's main international airport, Ezeiza Ministro Pistarini (EZE; ☎ 11/5480-9538), is 35km (22 miles) west of Buenos Aires. Travel to downtown takes from 45 minutes to more than an hour. There is no rail service from the airport. Taxis and *remises* (licensed minicabs) to downtown and Palermo cost AR$98 to AR$130. Do not accept transportation services from any private individuals; there is a well-organized booth ("Taxi Oficial Ezeiza") just after you exit Customs. They will ask what neighborhood you're headed to and organize a taxi; pay in either US dollars or Argentine pesos. Manuel Tienda León (☎ 11/4315-5115; www.tiendaleon.com.ar) offers dependable *remises* (car services; AR$120) and a bus service (AR$45) leaving every half hour.

Getting **Around**

By Subte (Subway)
The Buenos Aires *subte* (☎ 11/
4555-1616; www.subte.com.ar), or
subway—Latin America's first—is
very inexpensive and a pretty effi-
cient way to get around. However,
not all parts of the city are accessible by *subte* (the Recoleta, Palermo
Viejo, and Puerto Madero neighborhoods principal among them), and
most of the subway system is very
crowded at almost all hours of the
day and insufferably hot; even
newer cars lack air-conditioning. Six
subte lines operate Monday through
Saturday from 5am to 11pm and
Sunday and holidays from 8am to
10:30pm. The flat fare is AR$1.10. If
you're using the *subte* frequently,
purchase a credit card–like
monedero that functions with an
electronic reader; you can put any
amount you like on the card and use
it like a debit card (while you won't
save any money, you will avoid waiting in lines). Even if you don't much
use the *subte* for transportation,
you should ride at least once on the
original 1913 wooden cars of the A
line that run beneath Av. de Mayo.

By Taxi
Buenos Aires has nearly as many
black-and-yellow taxis in the street
as Manhattan, and fares are inexpensive compared with other major
cities. Because robberies in taxis
hailed on the street are not uncommon, it's most advisable to call (or
have your hotel or restaurant call) a
remise or radio-taxi (if you do hail
a taxi in the street, look for one with
a rooftop light box and a car that
says "radio taxi" and has a dis-
patcher phone number on the
door). Few taxi rides in Buenos Aires
will cost more than US$5 to US$8.
To request a reliable and safe taxi

by phone, call Radio Taxi Premium
(☎ 11/4374-6666), Pídalo (☎ 11/
4956-1200), or Remises Blue (☎ 11/
4777-8888).

By Bus
City buses are referred to as colecti-
vos, and there are 140 bus lines
operating 24 hours a day. However,
for most visitors, buses aren't a
great or even good option because
routes are very hard to decipher
and, unless you know the city very
well, you're likely to get lost. The
minimum fare is AR$1; you pay
inside the bus at an electronic ticket
machine, which accepts coins only
but gives change. Long-distance
buses to San Antonio de Areco and
other destinations beyond the capital leave from Estación Terminal de
Omnibus, Av. Ramos Mejía 1680
(☎ 11/4310-0700; www.tebasa.
com.ar), near Retiro Station (and
thus often called "Estación Retiro").

By Car
A car should only be used to get out
of town, not for transportation
within the capital. Traveling by
subte (subway), taxi, or *remise*
(licensed minicab) is much more
convenient, safer, and less expensive than driving. See p 163 for
information on car rentals. The
Automóvil Club Argentino (ACA),
Av. del Libertador 1850 (☎ 11/
4802-6061) has arrangements with
international automobile clubs and
offers roadside assistance, maps,
and other information. Fuel (nafta)
costs just under US$1 per liter (about
US$4/gal.).

On Foot
While the city is much too extensive
for walking from neighborhood to
neighborhood, if you're concentrating on certain barrios, traveling on

foot is a good way to get around and get the feel of the city. The streets of Palermo (with its many parks and tree-lined streets), Palermo Viejo, Recoleta, and Puerto Madero are all perfect (and safe) for walkers. In addition, Av. de Mayo (in Monserrat) and the walking circuit of the neighborhood Abasto are also best explored on foot.

Fast **Facts**

APARTMENT RENTALS For families or long-term stays in Buenos Aires, the following are good resources: BA Apartments, with apartments throughout Buenos Aires, including the most desirable neighborhoods (☎ 11/4864-8084; www.ba apartments.com.ar); Base Buenos Aires, focusing on apartment rentals in the Palermo neighborhood (☎ 11/4865-1735; www.buenos airesbase.com); Best Rentals Buenos Aires, for affordable and budget long-term and short-term rentals (☎ 646/502-8639 in the U.S. and Canada, or 11/4833-9563; www. bestrentalsba.com); ByT Argentina, a service with apartments all over Buenos Aires, including many in Palermo Viejo (☎ 11/4876-5000; www. bytargentina.com); Friendly Apartments, offering gay-friendly, short-term rentals with concierge and maid service (☎ 619/841-0054 in the U.S. and Canada, or 11/4816-9056; www.friendlyapartments. com); and Temporary Apartments, owned by the company behind Friendly Apartments (above), but appealing to a wider audience (☎ 619/841-0054 in the U.S. and Canada, or 11/4816-9032. www. temporaryapartments.com.ar).

ATMS/CASHPOINTS Maestro, Cirrus, and Visa cards are readily accepted at all ATMs, which dispense cash in pesos only. Exchange currency either at banks or casas de cambio (exchange houses). You can also find currency exchange offices at the San Martín rail station and Ezeiza airport. Most banks offer 24-hour ATMs; look for the Banelco or Link signs, but be very careful, especially at night, as ATM robberies are not uncommon.

BUSINESS HOURS Banks are open weekdays from 10am to 3pm. Shopping hours are weekdays from 9am to 8pm and Saturday from 9am to 2pm (though in most tourist areas until 6pm). Shopping centers are open daily from 10am to 10pm. A few smaller shops still close for lunch, though this is becoming more of a rarity.

CONSULATES & EMBASSIES Canadian Embassy, Tagle 2828, Palermo (☎ 11/4808-1000; www.dfait-maeci.gc.ca); U.S. Embassy, Av. Colombia 4300, Palermo (☎ 11/5777-4533; http://argentina.us embassy.gov); Australian Embassy, Villanueva 1400, Belgrano (☎ 11/4779-3500; www.argentina.embassy. gov.au); New Zealand Embassy, Carlos Pellegrini 1427, 5th floor, Retiro (☎ 11/4328-0747; www.nzembassy. com/buenosaires); United Kingdom Embassy, Luis Agote 2412, Recoleta (☎ 11/4808-2200; http://ukin argentina.fco.gov.uk).

DOCTORS For an English-speaking doctor, call Hospital Alemán (☎ 11/4827-7000), Hospital Británico (☎ 11/4309-6400), or Blue Care (☎ 11/4822-7244), the last for doctor house calls.

ELECTRICITY Electricity in Argentina is 220 volts. There are two kinds of outlets: the round two-prong

European-style, and a slanted flat-prong style unique to Argentina and Uruguay. Adapters are available throughout the city.

EMERGENCIES For an ambulance (free), call ☎ 107; in case of fire, call ☎ 100; for police assistance, call ☎ 101. All are free calls from any phone. The Comisaría del Turista, or tourist police (☎ 800/999-0500) is located at Av. Corrientes 436 (between San Martín and Reconquista).

GAY & LESBIAN TRAVELERS Argentina is a traditional, Catholic country and not the most progressive nation in terms of homosexuality, though Buenos Aires is in large part an exception; the city has become something of a haven for gay travelers in South America. Buenos Aires was the first major Latin American city to enact a Civil Union law for gay and lesbian couples (in 2003). San Telmo is emerging as the leading gay-friendly neighborhood, with Barrio Norte a close second. Across the city, there are restaurants, bars, nightclubs, and tango salons that are not only gay-friendly, but which specifically cater to the gay and lesbian community. See www.gayin buenosaires.com.ar for additional information.

HOLIDAYS Public holidays observed are January 1 (New Year's Day), Good Friday, May 1 (Labor Day), May 25 (First Argentine Government), June 10 (National Sovereignty Day), June 20 (Flag Day), July 9 (Independence Day), August 17 (Anniversary of the Death of General San Martín), October 12 (Día de la Raza), December 8 (Immaculate Conception Day), and December 25 (Christmas Day).

INSURANCE Check your existing insurance policies before you buy travel insurance to cover trip cancellation, lost luggage, medical expenses, or car rental insurance.

For more information, contact one of the following recommended insurers: Access America (☎ 866/807-3982; www.accessamerica. com); Travel Guard International (☎ 800/826-4919; www.travelguard. com); Travel Insured International (☎ 800/243-3174; www.travel insured.com); and Travelex Insurance Services (☎ 888/457-4602; www.travelex-insurance.com). For travel overseas, most U.S. health plans (including Medicare and Medicaid) do not provide coverage, and the ones that do often require payment for services upfront. If you require additional medical insurance, try MEDEX Assistance (☎ 410/453-6300; www.medexassist.com) or Travel Assistance International (☎ 800/821-2828; www.travel assistance.com; for general information on services, call the company's Worldwide Assistance Services, Inc., at ☎ 800/777-8710).

INTERNET Internet access is widely available, in cybercafes, bars/restaurants, and hotels, many of which offer Wi-Fi. Access is reasonably priced (usually about US$1/hr. or less), and connections are reliable. To find cybercafes in Buenos Aires, check www.cybercaptive.com and www.cybercafe.com.

LOST PROPERTY Call credit card companies the minute you discover your wallet has been lost or stolen and file a report at the nearest police precinct. Your credit card company or insurer may require a police report number or record. Visa's North America emergency number is ☎ 800/847-2911, or 11/4379-3333 in Buenos Aires. American Express cardholders and traveler's check holders should call ☎ 800/221-7282 in North America or 810/444-2484 in Argentina. MasterCard holders should call ☎ 800/307-7309 in North America, or

800/555-0507 or 11/4378-7070 in Buenos Aires.

MAIL & POSTAGE Post offices are open weekdays from 8am to 8pm and Saturday from 10am to 1pm. The main post office (Correo Central) is at Av. Sarmiento 151 (☎ 11/4316-3000).

MONEY Argentina's currency is the peso. At press time, the exchange rate was approximately US$1 = AR$3.5. For up-to-the-minute exchange rates, check the currency converter website www.xe.com/ucc.

PASSPORTS Citizens of the United States, Canada, the United Kingdom, Australia, New Zealand, and South Africa require a passport to enter Argentina. No visa is required for citizens of these countries for tourist stays of up to 90 days. If your passport is lost or stolen, contact your country's embassy or consulate immediately. See "Consulates & Embassies," above. Make a copy of your passport's critical pages and keep that copy separate from your passport.

PHARMACIES Pharmacies (farmácias) operate during normal business hours, and one in every district remains open all night and on holidays. The location and phone number of this farmácia de turno is posted on the door of all the other pharmacies. The largest branch is called FarmaCity, with 87 branches across the city, many open 24 hours. One is at Florida 474 (☎ 11/4322-6559; www.farmacity.com).

POLICE For police assistance, call ☎ 101. The Comisaría del Turista, or tourist police (☎ 800/999-0500), is located at Av. Corrientes 436 (between San Martín and Reconquista).

SAFETY Petty crime is a concern in Buenos Aires, especially during economically uncertain times. Look out for pickpockets and purse-snatchers on the streets and subways, buses, and trains. Professional-looking cameras attract a lot of attention, so handle your camera and lenses with great care when out in public (especially tourist haunts, like San Telmo). Avoid particularly contentious demonstrations, strikes, and other political gatherings, and avoid hailing taxis in the street (call for a radio-taxi instead). Some barrios should be considered unsafe at night: Monserrat (away from Av. de Mayo), La Boca/Constitución, and some sections of San Telmo (which today is much safer than it has been in years past). The Comisaría del Turista, or tourist police (☎ 800/999-0500), is located at Av. Corrientes 436 (between San Martín and Reconquista) and is open 24 hours.

SMOKING Although an antismoking law was passed in 2006, banning smoking in most public places, nicotine fixes remain a fundamental part of life in Buenos Aires. Relatively few restaurants have smoking and nonsmoking sections; if you feel strongly about avoiding secondhand smoke, ask establishments if they have a no fumadores (nonsmoking) section.

TAXES Argentina's value added tax (VAT), abbreviated as IVA, is 21%. Non-residents can recover 17.35% at the airport on purchases totaling more than AR$70 (per invoice) from stores participating in tax-free shopping. Ask when making purchases or look for the TAX-FREE or GLOBAL REFUND sign in the store's window. Forms, obtained from the store where you made your purchase, must be stamped at Customs upon departure. For more information, see www.globalrefund.com. The whopping 21% tax surcharge on hotel rates is not refundable.

TELEPHONES   Dial ☎ 110 for information, ☎ 000 to reach an international operator. To make an international call, dial ☎ 00, wait for the tone, and dial the country code, area code, and local number. If you're making a local call, dial the two-digit city code first and then the eight-digit number. To dial another number in Argentina from Buenos Aires, dial the area code first, then the local number. The city area code for Buenos Aires is 11 (from outside the capital, dial 0 + 11). A 15 in front of a local number indicates a cellphone. The easiest way to place international calls is by going to a *locutorio* (call center). Pay for the call after speaking (direct dial). You can also use a pre-paid calling card, available at kiosks, for calls from coin-operated public phones.

TIPPING   A 10% tip is expected at cafes and restaurants (15% for better service). Give at least AR$2 to bellboys and porters, and leftover change to taxi drivers by rounding up to the nearest peso. Leave about a US$1 a day for maid service at hotels, more in upscale places.

TOILETS   In Argentina, they're called baños or servicios, and are labeled caballeros or H (for hombre) for men and damas or M (for mujer) for women.

TOURIST INFORMATION   Tourism Information Centers offer maps, brochures, and limited information in several neighborhoods. Centro: Florida 100 (Mon–Fri 10am–6pm, Sat 10am–4pm); Retiro: Plaza San Martín, Florida at Marcelo T. de Alvear (Mon–Sat 10am–6pm); Puerto Madero: Alicia Moreau de Justo 200, Dique 4 (daily 10am–6pm); San Telmo: Defensa 1250 (Mon–Fri 10am–5pm, Sat & Sun 10am–6pm); and Recoleta: Quintana 596 (daily 10am–6pm). The Buenos Aires City Tourism Office has a toll-free tourist assistance line (☎ 800/999-2838) for complaints, staffed daily from 9am to 8pm.

TRAVELERS WITH DISABILITIES   Buenos Aires can be a frustrating destination for travelers with disabilities. The *subte* is not equipped for such travelers, nor are most buses. Although many larger upscale hotels have a rooms designed for travelers with disabilities, you should ask pointed questions in advance of making reservations, as the concept of being accessible is not universally applied. Two stylish hotels of note, Hotel Home (p 141) and 725 Continental Hotel (p 144), have disabled-access rooms. A guide to "accessible tourism," with detailed information on tours, museums, hotels, restaurants, theaters, and more, is available (in PDF format and in Spanish) at www.bue.gov.ar. For additional information, call ☎ 800/999-2838.

A Brief **History**

<table>
<tr><td>1536</td><td>Pedro de Mendoza (c. 1487–1537), a Spanish conquistador, arrives with 1,600 troops and establishes the first settlement—which he named "Nuestra Señora del Buen Ayre"—near Parque Lezama in San Telmo.</td></tr>
<tr><td>1541</td><td>Settlement abandoned due to starvation and conflict with natives.</td></tr>
<tr><td>1580</td><td>The second, and lasting, founding of the city by Juan de Garay (1528–1583), who arrived from Asunción and called the site (near current Plaza de Mayo)</td></tr>
</table>

"Santísima Trinidad y Puerto Santa María de los Buenos Aires."

1633   Jesuits establish intellectual heart of the city, Manzana de las Luces.

1680   Spanish government encourages the growth of Buenos Aires to keep pace with the Portuguese, who've established a trading post across the Río de la Plata.

1776   Spain creates Viceroyalty of Río de la Plata (which encompassed modern-day Paraguay, Uruguay, and Argentina) and names Buenos Aires capital.

1806   English forces invade the city in unsuccessful attempt to seize control.

1810   Revolución de Mayo: Provisional, independent government formed after Viceroyalty overthrown in first step towards independence.

1811–1820   Civil war over provincial autonomy.

1816   9 de Julio: Political independence formally declared.

1829   Juan Manuel de Rosas (1793–1877) assumes power and rules repressive dictatorship for 23 years.

1852   Rosas overthrown in revolt led by General Justo José de Urquiza (1801–1870).

1856   First Constitution drafted and Federalist system imposed.

1862   First president of Argentine Republic, Bartólome Mitre (1821–1906), elected.

1871   Yellow fever epidemic sweeps through San Telmo, killing 13,000 and forcing city's elite to flee north to Recoleta.

1880   The beginning of a Golden Age of immigration and expansion of the city; more than 3 million Spaniards, Italians, Syrian-Lebanese, Poles, and Russians immigrate between 1880 and 1914.

1883   Torcuator de Alvear (1822–1890), the city's first mayor, institutes grand urban plan with French-style boulevards.

1886   Buenos Aires named the capital of the Argentine Republic.

1894   Grand avenue Avenida de Mayo links Plaza de Mayo with the Congressional Palace.

1913   Subway system introduced, first in Latin America.

1914   Carlos Gardel (1890–1935) makes debut as a tango singer.

1914–1918   Argentine economy flourishes during World War I and increased world demand for agricultural products.

1943   After military coup, Juan Perón (1895–1974) becomes Minister of Labor.

1946   Perón assumes presidency; reelected 1951.

1952   Perón's wife, the first lady Eva Perón (1919–1952), known affectionately as Evita, dies of cancer.

1955   Perón overthrown and escapes into exile.

1973   Perón returns to Argentina from exile and elected president for third time.

1974   Perón dies in office; second wife, Isabelita (1931–), also vice president, assumes the presidency.

1976   Violent military coup led by General Jorge Videla (1925–); "National Reorganization

The Art of Porteño Speak

Although Argentines call their version castellano (Castilian), Argentine Spanish is unlike the Spanish spoken in Spain or anywhere else in Latin America. Argentina's large Italian immigrant population left a huge impression on the language, lending it a distinct flavor and rhythm. Certain usages exist only in Argentina. Rather than employ the informal form for you (*tú,* used throughout Latin America and Spain), Argentines say *vos*. And they conjugate the second-person familiar in a way all their own. Instead of *"tú que haces?"* (what are you doing?), Argentines say *"vos que hacés?"* with the accent on the second syllable. Another very distinctive feature of Argentine Spanish is the pronunciation of the double "l" in words like *parrilla* and "y" in words such as *playa*. Instead of the "yeh" sound found in both cases in the rest of Latin America and Spain, Argentines say "zheh," as in the word "azure."

Argentines are also well known for their vibrant use of local slang, called *lunfardo,* a street language you'll hear nowhere else (many words are derivative of Italian). *Che* is one of the most popular and recognizably Argentine terms, and not just because it was the nickname of that legendary revolutionary Che Guevara, who left a comfortable Argentine upbringing to foment social and political upheaval in Cuba and Bolivia. *Che* is an informal way of addressing an acquaintance; though it's been around for decades, it's more or less the equivalent of the current English-language "dude." Attractive young women are called *minas,* young men are *pibes*. A bus, ordinarily called a *colectivo,* is also a *bondi;* a taxi is called a *tacho,* the driver a *tachero.* A police officer? *La cana* or *yuta.* A friend: *gomia.* Work is *laburo,* money is *guita, morfar* is to eat, and *curda* is to be drunk as a skunk. Shoes are *timbos, pilchas* are clothes, and something *trucho* is poor quality. If you already speak some Spanish, getting a grip on Argentine Spanish is something else entirely, and it only begins with the accent, *che!*

Process" institutes country-wide censorship and repression, suspending much of the Constitution; beginning of "Dirty War" against suspected subversives and students that results in the disappearance of 30,000 citizens.

1977   Madres de la Plaza de Mayo protest movement founded.

1980   Human rights activist Adolfo Pérez Esquivel (1931–) wins Nobel Peace Prize.

1982   Military invades Falkland Islands (held by the British but known to Argentines as Las Malvinas); England defeats Argentina in the War of the South Atlantic, hastening fall of Argentine military junta.

1983   Return to democracy, as Raúl Alfonsín (1927–2009) elected president; Argentina begins investigation of the "Dirty War" and charges former military leaders with human rights abuses; inflation spirals to nearly 1,000%.

1986 Jorge Luis Borges (1899–1986), Argentina's most famous writer, dies.

1989 Carlos Ménem (1930–), of the Peronista party, elected president after Alfonsín steps down ahead of schedule.

1992 New Argentine currency, the peso, pegged to the U.S. dollar at 1:1.

1994 Jewish community center in Buenos Aires bombed, killing 86 people and injuring 200.

1995 Argentina becomes a member of the Southern Cone common market (Mercosur), along with Brazil, Uruguay, and Paraguay.

2001 Demonstrations, strikes, and fears of a devaluation of the peso lead to massive run on banks; President Fernando de la Rúa (1937–) declares state of emergency, then he and cabinet resign after 25 die in street protests.

2002 Peso devalued amid worsening economic crisis; banking and foreign exchange activity suspended; political chaos ensues with four presidents in less than 6 months.

2003 Nestor Kirchner (1950–) sworn in as president; economy rebounds to 5% annual growth.

2004 Judge issues international arrest warrant for former President Carlos Ménem, over allegations of fraud.

2004 Former President Carlos Ménem returns from self-imposed exile in Chile after cancellation of two arrest warrants.

2005 President Kirchner declares restructuring of national debt a success.

2006 Argentina repays multi-billion-dollar debt to International Monetary Fund.

2006 Violence erupts when remains of former President Perón transferred to new mausoleum outside capital.

2007 Cristina Fernández de Kirchner (1953–) elected president, succeeding her husband.

2008 Two former generals sentenced to life imprisonment for their roles in the "Dirty War."

2008 Pension funds nationalized.

Useful Words & Phrases

ENGLISH	SPANISH	PRONUNCIATION
Good day	Buenos días	bweh-nohs dee-ahs
How are you?	¿Cómo está?/¿Qué tal?	koh-moh es-tah/ kay-tahl
Very well	Muy bien	mwee byehn
Thank you	Gracias	grah-see-ahs
You're welcome	De nada	deh nah-dah
Goodbye	Adiós	ah-dyos
Please	Por favor	por fah-vohr
Yes	Sí	see
No	No	noh

ENGLISH	SPANISH	PRONUNCIATION
Excuse me	Perdóneme	pehr-doh-neh-meh
Where is . . . ?	¿Dónde está . . . ?	dohn-deh es-tah
To the right	A la derecha	ah lah deh-reh-chah
To the left	A la izquierda	ah lah ees-kyehr-dah
I would like . . .	Quisiera	kee-syeh-rah
I want . . .	Quiero	kyeh-roh
Do you have . . . ?	¿Tiene usted . . . ?	tyeh-neh oo-sted
How much is it?	¿Cuánto cuesta?	kwahn-toh kwehs-tah
When?	¿Cuándo?	kwahn-doh
What?	¿Qué?	Keh
There is (Is there . . . ?)	(¿)Hay (. . . ?)	aye
What is there?	¿Qué hay?	keh aye
Yesterday	Ayer	ah-yehr
Today	Hoy	oy
Tomorrow	Mañana	mah-nyah-nah
Good	Bueno	bweh-noh
Bad	Malo	mah-loh
Better (Best)	(Lo) Mejor	(loh) meh-hohr
More	Más	mahs/mehss
Less	Menos	meh-nohs
Do you speak English?	¿Habla inglés?	ah-blah een-glehs
I speak a little Spanish	Hablo un poco de español	ah-bloh oon poh-koh deh es-pah-nyol
I don't understand	No entiendo	noh ehn-tyehn-doh
What time is it?	¿Qué hora es?	keh oh-rah ehss
The check, please	La cuenta, por favor	lah kwehn-tah pohr fah-vohr
The station	La estación	lah es-tah-syohn
A hotel	Un hotel	oon oh-tehl
The market	El mercado	ehl mehr-kah-doh
A restaurant	Un restaurante	oon rehs-tow-rahn-teh
The toilet	El baño	ehl bah-nyoh
A doctor	Un médico	oon meh-dee-koh
The road to . . .	El camino a	ehl kah-mee-noh ah
To eat	Comer	ko-mehr
A room	Una habitación	oo-nah ah-bee-tah-syohn
A book	Un libro	oon lee-broh
A dictionary	Un diccionario	oon deek-syoh-nah-ryoh

Numbers

NUMBER	SPANISH	PRONUNCIATION
1	uno	oo-noh
2	dos	dohs
3	tres	trehs
4	cuatro	kwah-troh
5	cinco	seen-koh
6	seis	says

NUMBER	SPANISH	PRONUNCIATION
7	siete	syeh-teh
8	ocho	oh-choh
9	nueve	nweh-beh
10	diez	dyess
11	once	ohn-say
12	doce	doh-say
13	trece	treh-say
14	catorce	kah-tohr-say
15	quince	keen-say
16	dieciséis	dyeh-see-says
17	diecisiete	dyeh-see-syeh-teh
18	dieciocho	dyeh-see-oh-choh
19	diecinueve	dyeh-see-nweh-beh
20	veinte	bayn-teh
30	treinta	trayn-tah
40	cuarenta	kwah-rehn-tah
50	cincuenta	seen-kwehn-tah
60	sesenta	seh-sehn-tah
70	setenta	seh-tehn-tah
80	ochenta	oh-chehn-tah
90	noventa	noh-behn-tah
100	cien	seehn

Recommended **Argentine Wines**

Except for a very small number of elite French and Spanish restaurants, restaurants in Buenos Aires stock exclusively Argentine wines. And that's a good thing, given Argentina's recent explosive rise in prestige and popularity in the wine world. Visitors now have access to more red and white wines than ever before, including bottles from a growing number of boutique producers. Argentina has become the fifth-largest wine producer in the world, and according to most observers in South America, it has vaulted past Chile, the traditional leader. Although wine has been produced in Argentina since the 16th and 17th centuries, only recently has the rest of the world become familiar with Argentine wines (the country only began exporting its wine to other countries in any great number in the 1990s). Argentine wines are considered excellent values, and while that is still true for many, prices for premium wines have risen steadily and many wines are actually more expensive in Argentina than in your home country. The post-peso devaluation days of excellent $7 bottles in restaurants—it was tough to spend more than $15 for a top bottle in a chic restaurant as recently as 2006—look to be long gone. Still, there are some very fine wine values to be had, and Buenos Aires restaurants of all stripes—not just the celebrated *parrilladas*—offer great opportunities to explore Argentina's rapidly improved wines.

Reds (vinos tintos)

Argentina has latched on to its signature red grape, malbec, the varietal that dominates the Argentine wine industry. **Malbec** was originally primarily a blending grape in Bordeaux and Cahors, France, but in Argentina it has reached new heights. No other country produces malbecs on a competing level. With distinctive dark-fruit flavors of blackberry, black cherry, and plum, as well as mint, it produces a dark, medium-bodied, round, and jammy red wine—making it ideal for all the red meat and asados that Argentines love so much. Most of the best malbecs come from Mendoza, a high-altitude growing region in western Argentina (and producer of 80% of the country's wine), though some newer, excellent competition is coming from Patagonia, in the south, and Cafayate, in the north. **Cabernet sauvignon** ranks second among single-varietal wines, and Argentina also produces a significant amount of **syrah** and **merlot.** Malbecs have caught on in a big way, but many visitors are most enamored of blends with malbec as the principal varietal combined with cabernet sauvignon, cabernet franc, and merlot, as well as lesser-known grapes like bonarda and tannat.

Whites (vinos blancos)

The indigenous **torrontés** (tohr-ohn-tays) grape—grown only in Argentina—is quickly becoming the country's signature white wine, even if it hasn't caught up to malbec in terms of familiarity or renown. Though it is intensely aromatic and floral, with a jasmine and geranium nose that would seem to presage a sweet wine, torrontés is in fact a dry and crisp white. The flavor profile can exhibit white peach, mango, grapefruit, and pineapple notes, with lively acidity and occasionally a spicy edge. It comes off as something of a cross among muscat, viognier, and gewurztraminer. The best torrontés wines come from northern Argentina, especially Cafayate (a high-altitude, desert area near Salta). Torrontés is an excellent accompaniment for Asian and spicy foods, and especially that northern Argentine classic, the empanada. Less exalted but even more common whites in Argentina are medium-weight **chardonnay** (both aged in oak and steel-fermented) and fresh, light-bodied **sauvignon blanc;** Argentina also produces smaller quantities of **viognier** and **semillón.**

Toll-Free Numbers & Websites

AER LINGUS
☎ 800/474-7424 in the U.S.
☎ 01/886-8844 in Ireland
www.aerlingus.com

AEROLINEAS ARGENTINAS
☎ 800/333-0276 in the U.S.
☎ 800/688-0008 in Canada
☎ 0810/222-86527 in Argentina
www.aerolineas.com.ar

AIR CANADA
☎ 888/247-2262
www.aircanada.ca

AIR FRANCE
☎ 800/237-2747 in the U.S.
☎ 0820/820-820 in France
www.airfrance.com

AIR NEW ZEALAND
☎ *800/262-1234 or 800/262-2468 in the U.S.*
☎ *800/663-5494 in Canada*
☎ *0800/737-000 in New Zealand*
www.airnewzealand.com

ALITALIA
☎ *800/223-5730 in the U.S.*
☎ *8488/65641 in Italy*
www.alitalia.it

AMERICAN AIRLINES
☎ *800/433-7300*
www.aa.com

AUSTRIAN AIRLINES
☎ *800/843-0002 in the U.S.*
☎ *43/(0)5-1789 in Austria*
www.aua.com

BMI
☎ *0870/6070-222 in Britain*
www.flybmi.com

BRITISH AIRWAYS
☎ *800/247-9297 in the U.S.*
☎ *0870/850-9850 in Britain*
www.british-airways.com

CONTINENTAL AIRLINES
☎ *800/525-0280*
www.continental.com

DELTA AIR LINES
☎ *800/221-1212*
www.delta.com

EASYJET
☎ *0871/244 2366*
www.easyjet.com

IBERIA
☎ *800/772-4642 in the U.S.*
☎ *902/400-500 in Spain*
www.iberia.com

ICELANDAIR
☎ *800/223-5500 in the U.S.*
☎ *354/50-50-100 in Iceland*
www.icelandair.is

KLM
☎ *800/374-7747 in the U.S.*
☎ *020/4-747-747 in the Netherlands*
www.klm.nl

LAN
☎ *866/435-9526 in the U.S.*
☎ *810/999-9526 in Argentina*
www.lan.com

LUFTHANSA
☎ *800/645-3880 in the U.S.*
☎ *49/(0)-180-5-838426 in Germany*
www.lufthansa.com

NORTHWEST AIRLINES
☎ *800/225-2525*
www.nwa.com

QANTAS
☎ *800/227-4500 in the U.S.*
☎ *612/131313 in Australia*
www.qantas.com

SCANDINAVIAN AIRLINES
☎ *800/221-2350 in the U.S.*
☎ *0070/727-727 in Sweden*
☎ *70/10-20-00 in Denmark*
☎ *358/(0)20-386-000 in Finland*
☎ *815/200-400 in Norway*
www.scandinavian.net

SWISS INTERNATIONAL AIRLINES
☎ *877/359-7947 in the U.S.*
☎ *0848/85-2000 in Switzerland*
www.swiss.com

UNITED AIRLINES
☎ *800/241-6522*
www.united.com

US AIRWAYS
☎ *800/428-4322*
www.usairways.com

VIRGIN ATLANTIC AIRWAYS
☎ *800/862-8621 in the continental U.S.*
☎ *0870/380-2007 in Britain*
www.virgin-atlantic.com

Index

See also Accommodations and Restaurant indexes, below.

Photo **Credits**

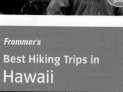

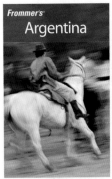